Dining Downunder

Series one

The Cook Book

Dining Downunder

Turning international cuisine upside down

Dining Downunder

Series one

The Cook Book

Vic Cherikoff

Benjamin Christie

Mark McCluskey

Dining Downunder

Turning international cuisine upside down

Published and distributed in Australia by
Dining Downunder Pty Ltd
ABN 74 103 225 207
rear 167 Kingsgrove Rd Kingsgrove NSW 2208

Email: info@dining-downunder.com
Website: www.dining-downunder.com

ISBN 0-9752021-0-3

For enquiries regarding distribution and sales,
please contact us on the email above.

Editors: Vic Cherikoff and Benjamin Christie

Food and studio photography by
Aussie Shots Sydney, Australia

Artwork and Design by
Aussie Shots

AUSSIE SHOTS
Imaging Synergy
www.aussieshots.com.au

Scenic photographs courtesy of Tourism New South Wales
and Australian Tourist Commission, James Christie and Queensland Tourism.

Table of contents

Preface

We are living in very exciting times. Most of us travel further in one year and know more people than our great grandparents did in their whole lifetimes. We are now exposed to more new ideas and more facts about world events than were our parents and our young are even learning new ways of viewing written words i.e. as screenfuls of conceptual information.

Our accelerated methods of learning and information exchange means that the food industry discovers new global trends, new products, innovations and applications in hours or days not years or generations.

For Australians, the Information Age offers huge potential. We have an emerging 'Australia' industry where our home-grown food resources are often showcased in presentations to a hungry international market. Unfortunately, government typically gets stuck on supply chain issues of the mechanics of food production and distribution rather than assisting the creation and management of the demand chain. This book and the television show from which it was spawned, aim to correct this imbalance as we showcase Australian products to the world.

Nevertheless, most Australian foodstuffs are perceived as clean, green, fresh and of high quality. (This may change as other genetically modified crops join canola, introduced at the ill-considered whim of government and pressure from foreign interests). There is added advantage in overseas markets as a result of their being Australian productions.Yet these are exotic products!

Authentically Australian foods which are indigenous to this country are now emerging as a significant force in the marketplace. Unlike some manufactured edibles on the market, native Australian ingredients are closer to nature than synthetic chemistry and they are distinctively different in their range of appealing tastes. We can now further differentiate menus and products in Australian restaurants and factories from those found anywhere else in the world. Authentic Australian ingredients and products made using them are filling niches throughout the food, tourism, hospitality and education industries and are ecologically friendly and culturally relevant foods which give a new meaning to being Australian.

A lot could be said about the organic methods employed in the agriculture of these foods or the involvement of Aboriginal communities in ecologically sustainable, wild harvests. More could be explained about the high nutritional density of indigenous foods or the discovery of the functional effects of specific constituents within them. But it is easier to picture diners in eateries anywhere on the planet, enjoying their local food styles with the inclusion of a few uniquely Australian flavours. Alternatively, imagine Australian chefs blending foreign cuisines and through the addition of our wild ingredients, make dishes which taste unlike those prepared with the same fusion styles by chefs in San Francisco, Tokyo, Singapore, New Zealand, London or even Dubai.

In a matter of years, I am convinced that we are set to create and enshrine in culinary tradition, an authentic Australian cuisine. It will be based upon ingredients native to this country, integrated into a multi-cultural food framework and include some Aboriginal cooking methods modified for the commercial kitchen. The tastes will reflect the vast outback, wild woodlands, lush rainforests, sweeping coastlines, sophisticated cities and quaint rural communities as well as the valuable natural and human resources of black and white Australians. Australia has a flavour and it's a wild one!

Vic Cherikoff
Joint Executive Producer, Dining Downunder

Lemon Aspen

Lemon Myrtle

Aniseed Myrtle

Quandong

Wild Limes

Muntries, Munthari

Kakadu Plum

A few words from Dick Smith ...

As a passionate supporter of all things Australian, I'm delighted to have the opportunity to introduce this fantastic book filled with recipes using authentic Australian ingredients, prepared by Vic Cherikoff and his team of expert chefs from the TV show "Dining Downunder".

Vic Cherikoff's passion for wild Australian foods is not just about the great tastes that can be found in the Aussie bush. Vic and many others, would love to see these incredible fruits, herbs, spices, nuts, seeds and more, make a contribution to the biodiversity of our farms and promote sustainable agriculture across Australia.

Vic and I share the dream that one day we might be able to travel country roads and look at bushland which is both productive with food and medicine species and presents a diverse habitat for more than just native animals and plants; but for ourselves as well.

Australians live in an amazing land which is slowly but surely being taken over by foreign interests, some of which may not understand or love our land or have our sense of the unique heritage that belongs to all Australians. Unfortunately, not everyone has the same sense of urgency to see the land thrive in a way that is economically, socially and environmentally sustainable.

I first became interested in food because I believe that Australians should remain involved in what takes place in their country, ensuring that a proper balance is maintained in the control and use of our natural resources. It is vital that Australians manage the land in a sustainable way; not out of self-interest but in the best interests of all who choose to live here. The food bounty our country can and does supply is a unique and important asset of the Australian landscape and should be nurtured.

This is embodied in the philosophy behind Dick Smith Foods – "good for all Australians and good for Australia". Our mission is to supply only top quality foods from Australian owned companies using Australian ingredients wherever possible. We will continue to explore ways in which Australian native foods can be incorporated into our products and invite all who may have an interest to try the unique taste experiences our land has on offer.

The recipes in this book include selected dishes from a range of restaurants, cafes and eateries in various parts of the country, chosen to reflect contemporary Australian cuisine available today.

These dishes are the inspiration for the chefs on "Dining Downunder" to put an authentic Australian twist to their interpretations of many traditional recipes, with many unique and new taste sensations on offer. The use of native Australian ingredients, along with the food tourism inclusions, should remind us of what it means to be Australian and what we can offer the world.

It is my hope that the unique taste experiences offered by our native species are a reminder of the unique place in which we live and how we can make an impact on the future of our land and its place on the global stage.

Dick Smith
Dick Smith Foods

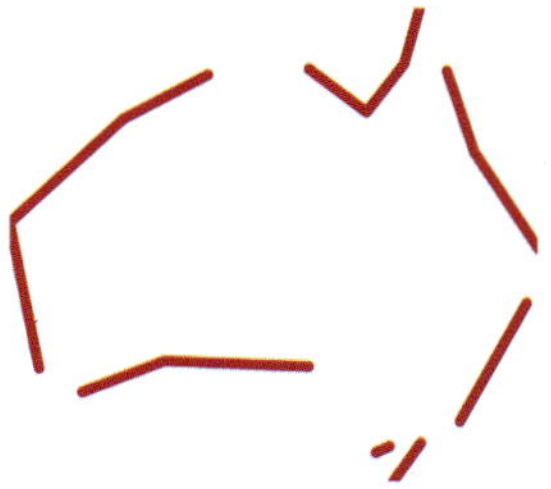

Some comments from Peter Woodland ...

It is often said that Australia does not have a distinct national cuisine. Our local cuisine is highly influenced by the many cultures that have settled here in this wonderful land over the last forty or so years. A term recently coined for this is 'Fusion cuisine' meaning the fusing of flavours and tastes from a diversity of cultures. And so, it could easily be argued that this is the true essence of what is 'Australian cuisine'.

In my travels abroad over the last 15 years, I have often asked people what they think is considered to be Australian cuisine and their responses have almost always been either 'meat pies' or 'barbecues'. (Wink!)

And even as recently as ten years ago, if you asked someone what they would expect to eat at a barbecue they would have almost always responded: "steaks or sausages". Today, of course, things are much, much different.

When I started BeefEater almost twenty years ago, I had a simple vision to develop a durable and dynamic gas barbecue inspired by the tough Australian environment. Having lived in both Europe and North America I knew our barbecue culture would be popular throughout the world. It had to be a real barbecue and not just a gas grill. A barbecue with versatility and leading edge technology using quartz and titanium, designed and built by Australians for the world.

As the market has grown both in Australia and abroad, consumer demand has became increasingly more sophisticated. Consumers no longer wanted just a simple rusty solid plate barbecue on which to cook the odd steak, snag or chop; they now wanted 'rust-free' technology to cook all sorts of foods on the barbecue to the same level of precision that they expected from the finest indoor kitchen appliances. And so, our strategy became one of innovation and technology. Today, BeefEater is a proudly Australian owned and operated company that manufactures and distributes barbecues both domestically and internationally.

Which brings us to our association with 'Dining Downunder'. About three years ago, the producers of the show approached us with a great concept about a uniquely Australian cooking and lifestyle show aimed at the international market. The team at Dining Downunder became immediately aware that a project of this genre would certainly not be complete without the inclusion of something so inextricably linked to Australian culture, 'the Aussie barbecue'. Of course, we immediately recognised this as a unique opportunity to not only showcase great Australian foods and flavours but also to show off some world class Australian made barbecues.

Today, people everywhere are becoming more informed about our unique Australian flavours because of the passion of people like Vic Cherikoff, who specialises in cooking using native Australian foods, foods which can't be found anywhere else in the world. As a result and because of shows like 'Dining Downunder', we can now truly understand and appreciate the different types of Australian flavours available to us. We can also learn how to incorporate these distinct flavours into our everyday cooking and cooking styles.

The flavours that are used in 'Dining Downunder' are uniquely Australian and the involvement of Australian indigenous people in the native food industry is a positive step in acknowledging their contribution to our modern food style. What better way to enhance this Australian experience than on a uniquely designed Australian BeefEater barbecue?

And so, we are immensely pleased and proud to support the team from 'Dining Downunder' with their vision of turning international cuisine upside down.

Peter Woodland
BeefEater Barbecues

DINING
DOWNUNDER

Dining
Downunder
www.dining-downunder.com

Some history from Grant Patterson ...

I was born in Hamilton, Ontario, Canada. When I was three years old, my family took in two young Australian men as boarders. They had quite an influence on my life as they told me about kangaroos, koalas, sharks, spiders, snakes, sheep and everything else about Australia. I was so interested in Australia that in 1971, I made the trip from Toronto to Sydney and within a week I was hired as a film checker at Sydney's Channel Seven television studios.

Back in the seventies it was practically impossible to find a good restaurant in Sydney. My impression of culinary Australia was pub grub and the local milk bars which featured meat pies, chiko rolls, dim sims, lambs brains and whatever else. My weirdest dining experience was at the Silver Spade Lounge at the Chevron Hilton Hotel. Bobbie Gentry, the one hit wonder (Ode to Billie Joe) was doing a show at the hotel and Channel Seven gave free tickets to its employees. The tickets included dinner and I thought that if nothing else, my friends and I would have a great meal so when the waiter arrived with a single bottle of beer and three plates featuring a potato pie and some peas I was a little shocked. I asked him what this was and he said "pie and peas, what the **** does it look like, it's your ****ing meal. Well that was then.

I came back to Australia in 1990 and discovered a whole new scene. Sydney had become a world class destination and fine restaurants were as diverse as they were plentiful. Aussie culture had managed a head-on collision with international cuisine and five star dining was a reality.

On another visit in 1997 and with the 2000 Olympics coming, I knew Australia would be the flavour of the next decade around the world but particularly in North America. I also thought that there should be a cooking show on the concept of 'Dining Downunder' to showcase Australia as a five star food and tourism destination. And so a new television show was conceived.

I started knocking on doors for sponsorship and it was tough. "We think it's a great idea but not at this time, call us back in a year or two", was the usual response. There was one Australian company that did come to the table and that was BeefEater BBQ. The series was another step closer to reality.

My search for more sponsors took me back and forth from Sydney to Melbourne and by the end of 2001 I was ready to give up. Throughout the four years of useless meetings and empty promises, I kept hearing of this, Vic Cherikoff person who knew "all about native flavours and foods". People described him to me in terms like, "he's a bit different" or "he's just a bit eccentric". My mind's eye conjured up visions of a mad Russian complete with a jet black eye brow, beard, wild hair, Rasputin-like eyes and he would speak with a Russian-Australian accent. I had already produced nearly four hundred episodes of a cooking show featuring a singing Italian chef and I had decided that an English speaking Australian was as ethnic as I intended to get. At my office in Melbourne in January 2002 as I made what I considered my last ditch phone calls, Vic's name came up again, not once but twice. I wrote down his phone number but decided against dealing with another eccentric.

I was in my office, packing my things in preparation for my return to Canada and listening for the local tram which stopped about four metres from the front door of my office. The screeching noise it made on its approach gave me a minute's warning. I was all packed when I heard the tram and I made my mad dash to the tram stop. It took me a little longer than usual this time, as I had to set the burglar alarm. When I finally got out the door I quickly moved toward the stop to flag the driver. He saw me and accelerated so by the time I got to the "Official Tram Stop" he had beaten me by a nose. He rang his bell and made a one fingered gesture as he laughingly sped away. With this extra twelve minutes I decide to make one last check of the office. As I sat down at my desk, I saw Vic's number and finally decided to give him a call. A conversation that I expected would last only a few minutes went on for over an hour. We met at his Sydney office the next day and I noted that he had two eye brows, bore no resemblance to Rasputin and spoke with an easy to understand Australian accent.

With Vic's knowledge of native Australian ingredients a new dimension was added to the series. Finally, Dining Downunder had a uniquely Australian flavour, literally! As he says: "On Dining Downunder, we take international cuisine and turn it upside down." And that's exactly what we are doing as we showcase Australia to the world. And all because of one government-trained tram driver.

Grant Patterson
Joint Executive Producer, Dining Downunder

We visited
a small
sandstone
cottage with
a long history
and now as
a modern
Australian
restaurant ....

Parramatta River

Recipes from Banjo Patterson Cottage Restaurant, Putney NSW

Charred beef tenderloin with braised wild mushrooms, macadamia and green beans

Serves 4

4 x 200g beef tenderloin
20ml olive oil
5g butter for frying
100g shiitake mushrooms
100g oyster mushrooms
100g Swiss brown mushrooms
40g chopped macadamia nuts
250g green beans
50g butter (kept cold)
80ml red wine
salt and pepper

1. Char grill the steaks on a BBQ or hot plate for 2 minutes; turn the steaks and cook to the desired doneness; a medium steak will take about 10 minutes depending on the size and temperature
2. once cooked, move to a warm place and allow to rest for at least 10 minutes
3. in a wok, heat a little oil and a teaspoonful of butter and sauté the mushrooms; add the macadamia nuts, salt and pepper
4. deglaze with a little red wine, turn the heat off, then add the cold butter to form a sauce
5. top and tail the beans and either blanch them or microwave until cooked but still crisp

Place the beans on the plate, then the beef on top of the beans. Spoon the mushrooms on top and drizzle the sauce on and around the beef.

Macadamia nougat ice cream

Serves 6

2 honey macadamia confectionery bars
6 egg whites
½ cup of sugar
250ml whipped cream
2 teaspoons sugarbag
2 punnets of raspberries

1. Coarsely chop up the macadamia nut bars
2. whip the egg whites and add sugar slowly
3. whip the cream and add the sugar bag
4. fold the macadamia nuts through the whipped cream
5. fold the egg whites through the cream mixture
6. line 6 moulds with plastic cling wrap
7. fill the moulds with the mixture and freeze for 2 - 3 hours

If the frozen nougats are difficult to remove from their moulds, dip the moulds into very hot water briefly. Remove the nougats, unwrap them and set in the middle of a dessert bowl. If the raspberries are sweet enough serve them as they come as a garnish; alternatively, tip them into a bowl sprinkle with superfine caster sugar and spray with hot water to dissolve the sugar onto the berries. Finally scatter them around the individual nougats.

Akudjura crusted ribeye steak
with wattleseed jus

If you can't find broccolini, use Chinese cabbage, asparagus or broccoli (slice the stems and some flowers lengthwise). Broccolini is an Australian horticultural cross between broccoli and Chinese kale. It has long edible stalks and more open florets than broccoli. ***BC***

Akudjura

Akudjura (pronounced with the accent on the CUD syllable) is an Anglicized version of an Aboriginal word for what is colloquially known as bush tomato or desert raisins (see pic below).

I have been out with Aboriginal women picking these small fruits from their prickly tomato-like bushes and marvel at the way the women can work for hours bent in half to reach the fruits. My back gives out after about 20 minutes of what I regard as really hard work or else I just have to sit down in the red dirt and pick away. It's a whole lot easier but heaps slower (and hotter).

Today, in contemporary usage, akudjura is a term given to the ground spice made from the milled dried fruits of the bush tomato. It has a tamarillo and caramel flavour.

serves 4

4 x 220g rib eye steak (scotch fillet)
1 tablespoons akudjura
50ml red wine
2 teaspoons wattleseed
100ml beef jus or rich beef stock
100g shiitake mushrooms
a generous pinch or two of Alpine Pepper
1 large bunch broccolini
½ teaspoon Rainforest Rub
4 sprigs watercress

1. Heat a pan to hot, add a little oil then place each steak into the pan; cook the first side until a light colour is achieved; do not turn the meat over at this stage
2. while the meat is searing, spread the akudjura with a little Outback salt and Alpine pepper onto a plate; then dip the cooked side of each steak into the mix, crusting the mix evenly on the cooked side of the steak
3. add a little more oil to the pan and return the steaks to the pan, crusted side down and allow the akudjura to caramelise slightly
4. repeat with the other side of the steaks
5. once cooked to the desired doneness, remove and allow to rest in a warm place for about 5 minutes; while the meat is resting, quickly prepare the broccolini and shiitake mushrooms
6. deglaze the pan juices with a little red wine, add the wattleseed and reduce; pour through a strainer and reserve the liquid in a small saucepan
7. add the beef jus to the reserved liquid and bring to a gentle simmer and reduce to around 80ml or until the vegetables are done; thicken with a slurry of corn flour or arrowroot if necessary
8. to the deglazed hot pan, add a little more oil and a nob of butter and toss in the shiitake mushrooms; season with the Alpine Pepper; remove when golden
9. re-oil the pan and quickly wok toss the broccolini until cooked; season with the Rainforest Rub

Use a medium sized main course plate; place the broccolini in the centre of the plate, put the steak on this and then the shiitake mushrooms on top; around the base of the plate pour the sauce; serve with a sprig of watercress

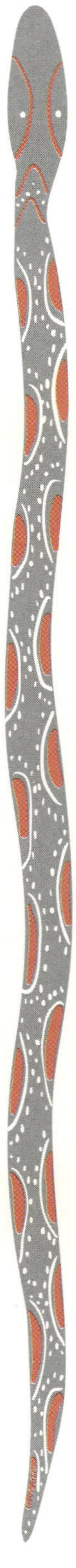

Braised chicken
in a sweet corn and polenta broth

Be bold with your flavours here. The Wildfire Spice adds almost pizza notes but you can get smokey flavours from the BBQ or crank up the chilli, if you like it hot! Also, any prosciutto can be used, pan-fried to crispness for what Vic calls that all-important, "textural crunch!" ***MM***

serves 4

4 x 100g chicken breast
1 teaspoon Wildfire Spice
Australian olive oil, as needed
3 cobs sweet corn
1 chilli, chopped
1 teaspoon minced ginger
2 litre chicken stock
200g polenta
100ml coconut cream
seasoning to taste
100g emu prosciutto
4 sprigs of watercress

1. Marinate the chicken breast in Wildfire Spice and olive oil
2. remove the corn from the husk and rub with olive oil; BBQ until tender
3. add some oil to a pan and briefly fry the ginger and chilli; add the chicken stock and bring to the boil
4. add the polenta, chicken and coconut cream and simmer for 5 minutes
5. remove the corn kernels from the cob and add them to the soup; simmer for 1 minute more
6. remove from the heat, check the seasoning and add more Wildfire Spice if required

Divide the broth into four medium sized soup plates. Garnish each with a sprig of watercress and finish with the emu prosciutto.

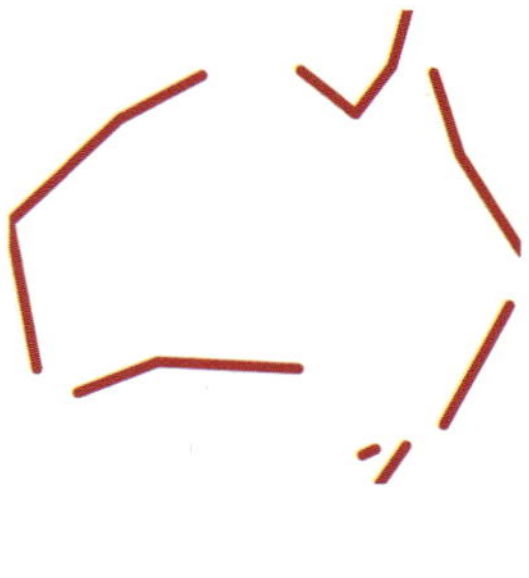

Boomerang trifle

with lemon ironwood syrup, wild fruit jelly and Fruit Spice cream

This dessert takes some forward planning with the jelly and fruit compote having to be made the day before. In fact, the cake is better if it's not just baked but a few days old and the cream will get stronger in taste overnight in the fridge as well. This dish also lends itself to a whole lot of improvisation; from sherry, brandy or ice wine for soaking the cake to wattleseed cream, gumleaf custard or Oz Lemon ice cream. ***VC***

serves 4

Madeira or butter cake, or use sponge if you must (too soft and fluffy for me)
100ml lemon ironwood syrup or use maple syrup and Oz lemon (see below)
red wine jelly crystals
a selection of red wild fruits e.g. wild rosella, riberries, Davidson plum
sugar as required
fresh blueberries, raspberries or whatever you can find easily
100ml thickened cream, whipped to firm peaks
¼ teaspoon Fruit Spice
lemon verbena leaves or mint for garnish

1. Cut the boomerang shape from an appropriately sized piece of the cake you are using and soak it in the syrup.
2. if you can't find lemon ironwood syrup, make this substitute; warm 100ml of maple syrup to around 44°C (that's about as hot as you can stand if you dip your finger in but be careful not to cook it – your finger that is); add ¼ teaspoon of Oz Lemon and leave to cool before soaking the cake
3. prepare the jelly according to the instructions on the pack, pour into an ice cube tray and leave to set
4. once ready to use, carefully remove the jelly from the tray by running a knife around the edges and cut the cubes into 4 smaller cubes
5. in a small saucepan, add the fruits and just cover with water; add about the same amount of sugar as for the weight of fruits and heat to dissolve the sugar and cook the fruits which should stay quite firm
6. add the Fruit Spice to the whipped cream and leave stand for at least an hour

Place the syrup soaked boomerang on a plate. Pile on the jelly cubes and spoon on the fruit compote and the fresh berries. Drizzle the cake with any left-over lemon ironwood syrup and place your dollop of Fruit Spice cream. Finally garnish with the leaves and serve immediately.

An average day for the Dining Downunder team on the job at NBN studios, Newcastle.

6:30am / 7:00 a.m. Wake up check emails

8:00am Breakfast in Breezes restaurant in Crown Plaza Newcastle. This is production meeting no.1 with cast and production staff able to surface from the early morning shooting (3am some days)

9:00am taxies and cars to NBN studios

9:15am Kitchen briefing with TAFE students detailing dishes for the days shoot (these guys and girls worked their tails off supporting us and we really appreciate and thank them for their efforts – we couldn't have done the show as easily without them)

10:00am Mark leads mise en place in the kitchen, Ben shopping for missing ingredients, Vic chasing finance for the show and keeping his food service business going, Grant desperately seeking a band as our musicians from Sydney never showed up. That's show business.

11:00am Production meeting No.2 outlining the day's episodes and finalising each episode's running sheets. Grant still looking for a band.

12:00pm Prep work continues amid organisation of set equipment, continuous washing up, restocking of ingredients, planning and etc

12:30pm Vic, Ben & Mark review ingredients and prepare for the first episode of the day. Clare organises table setting, glassware and table decorations to go with each dish as we plate up and for the last segment of each episode.

12:45pm Vic, Ben & Mark to make up and a laugh with Craig. The audience arrives at the studio.

1:00pm Cast and Crew all assemble in Studio B. It's the last chance to review the running sheet and make any changes to the episode or camera order. At the same time Vic, Ben and Mark all get wired up with microphones by the audio guys.

1:10pm Vic, Ben and Mark check and recheck equipment and ingredients. There're no knives on the set. What plates are we using? Where's that large mixing bowl gone? Who's doing the washing up? We need more hands on deck. Vic finds out what he is cooking for this episode, he also takes a minute or two to introduce the chefs to the audience and gives them an idea of what to expect.

1:12pm Vic dictates the details for each strap (the information which runs on the screen throughout the episodes)

1:14pm Grant finds someone for the audience to join us on stage for the final segment and more importantly, to try the food! They get wired for sound and a quick make up job.

1:25pm Lights. Camera. Action. The 1 minute opener rolls and the episode gets underway. Filming takes place until around 1:55pm and the cameras and crew disappear to Studio A for a quick taping of the local News at 6pm.

1:56pm All the dishes are quickly sent to the make shift photo studio for Geordie (our photographer)

to capture. He quickly styles, lights and shoots each dish as prepared for screen shots, this cookbook, our website, other publications and general PR. Few dishes escaped being tasted by Geordie. Some dishes like Vic's Wattleseed pavlova seemed to totally disappear and never made it back to the studio for the audience to try.

1:57pm The team of TAFE students clean down the set and re organise the ingredients and utensils for the next episode. Not much time between episodes. Grant, Clare, Vic, Ben and Mark have a quick look at the segments just filmed and decide if they are good enough to keep or if they have to be re filmed before progressing to the next episode.

2:15pm When the cameras come back we either re-take any bits and pieces from the previous episode or move on to the next. Filming goes through to 3:55pm when all the cameras are again required in Studio A for the news.

3:55pm Cast and crew take a break for dinner and to relax till the news is finished, about 6:45pm for a 7pm kick off. Vic goes back to chasing finance and Grant keeps hunting down a band.

6:00pm The kitchen is reset for the next set of filming and the chefs go back to makeup and it all starts again.

6:25pm A new audience is introduced and few audience members are selected for each episode.

6:30pm All the ingredients are checked as well as table setting, cooking utensils etc

6:45pm Cameras and crew are back from the news room and are ready to roll for the next episode.

7:00pm Lights. Camera. Action. Again. The 1 minute opener rolls and the next episode gets underway as though it was the first time for the day. Some segments get canned, some are 'in the can'. One went on until 3am but with a bit of luck, we aim to do 4 episodes a day – plan the shoot, prep the food, cook it off, clean up and prep again, punch them out; something goes wrong – we try it again. The idea though, is get it in one, shoot live to tape and remember, entertain the audience at the same time.

ARK
29

Executive Chef Matthew Harangozo fired up a treat for us as interesting as the view.

Blue Mountains

Recipes from the Hydro Majestic, Medlow Bath, Blue Mountains NSW

Pumpkin risotto

4 – 6 serves depending if entrée or main sized

400g Arborio rice
1 litre vegetable stock (see page 185)
100ml white wine
50g onion
2 cloves garlic
150g pumpkin
30g butter
1 bay leaf
6 asparagus spears
50g parmesan cheese
10g toasted macadamia nut pieces
10g salt
10ml white truffle oil

1. Peel and dice the pumpkin, place into cold water and bring to a boil until partially cooked but still firm; drain and dry on paper towelling; then sauté the pumpkin dice in a pan with a little oil, keeping the pan as hot as possible to caramelise the outside of the pumpkin and finish cooking it; drain onto paper towelling and reserve
2. finely dice the onion and mince the garlic
3. then, in small pot, melt the butter and sauté the garlic and onion
4. add the bayleaf and the rice, sautéing on low heat, until the rice grains become translucent
5. add 200ml of the vegetable stock and cook until the liquid is reduced, stirring constantly
6. continue to add vegetable stock in 200ml amounts, stirring and reducing until the liquid is absorbed and repeat; the final addition will be the white wine
7. all up, it will take about 25 minutes to cook until the rice is tender
8. trim the asparagus and cut into 8-9cm pieces – the tops of the spears will be used for garnish and the stems will be used in the risotto itself
9. lightly stir-fry the asparagus spears
10. remove the asparagus from the pan, set aside until the rice is cooked
11. once the rice is cooked add the pumpkin, chopped asparagus stems and some parmesan cheese; gently mix through, taste and add salt if required

To serve, place a mould on a plate, fill with risotto and lift the mould; place the stir fried asparagus spearheads on the risotto and sprinkle with toasted macadamia nuts and remaining parmesan cheese; finish with a drizzle of white truffle oil.

Morel mushroom pasta

Serves 4

200g shiitake mushrooms, finely sliced
250g fresh morel mushrooms (well washed to remove any sand)
500g pappardelle or fettuccini pasta
2 cloves garlic
100ml vegetable stock
1 onion
30g butter
400ml fresh cream
1 small tomato
100g grilled capsicum
60g snow peas
5g parsley, chopped
2ml black truffle oil

1. Place a pot of water on the stove for the pasta, add salt and a little oil to stop the pasta sticking; when the water begins to boil, add the pasta and cook until al denté (this is the Italian term used to describe any type of pasta that is cooked until tender but still slightly firm 'to the tooth')
2. once the pasta is cooked, drain all but 5% of the water through a colander and put the pasta back in the pot with this reserved water
3. meanwhile, finely chop and mince the garlic and slice the onion
4. melt a little butter in a pan and begin to slowly caramelise the onion and garlic
5. add the mushrooms, continuing on a slow heat, this allows the mushrooms to release all their flavour to the pan and which will form the basis of the rich sauce (add a dash of vegetable stock if the pan is a little dry)
6. slice the snow peas and grilled capsicum and dice the tomato
7. to finish the mushroom sauce; increase the temperature in the pan and add the cream, snow peas, capsicum, tomato and some of the chopped parsley; allow the sauce to reduce and add the pasta
8. taste the sauce and add a little sea salt, if necessary

Serve in a pasta bowl with the rest of the parsley and drizzle a little truffle oil over the top.

Mixed berry compote in crepes

Serves 4 - 6

Crepe mix

250g plain flour
a generous pinch of salt
30g sugar
2 eggs
500ml milk
50g butter

1. In a bowl or mixer combine the sugar and eggs and sift in the flour
2. pour in the milk to make a smooth batter
3. melt the butter, and then add the butter into the batter
4. strain the batter with a fine strainer to remove any lumps
5. leave the batter to sit for 20 minutes and adjust the consistency, if necessary; the batter can't be too thick, as it needs to fill the entire pan to form the crepe; so if it requires more milk add a little
6. heat the pan on a medium-high heat and keep in mind that the pan shouldn't be too oily; so it's best to either use spray oil or an oil soaked paper towel
7. pour in the mixture, and try to keep the crepe thin and almost transparent
8. when the mixture starts to bubble, its time to turn it over
9. generally the first one you make will be too oily or be too coloured; adjust the heat accordingly
10. re-oil the pan between crepes; cook both sides to just tan in colour and stack the crepes onto a plate as they are made and allow to cool

Mixed Berry Compote

2 granny smith apples
100g fresh or frozen raspberries
200g fresh or frozen blue berries
100 fresh or frozen blackberries
500g sugar

1. Peel and core the apples, and cut into 1cm dice
2. place about 75% of each of the berries and all of the apple dice into a small pot; stir and cook over a low heat; you may need a little water, but generally there will be enough liquid from the berries and apple
3. cook, stirring occasionally, until the fruit softens and then add the sugar; continue heating and stirring occasionally for about an hour or until combined as a jam, be sure to mix well from time to time
4. add the remaining berries which will stay whole and firm because of the sugar content in the jam; heat, stirring gently for another 5 minutes

To assemble the dish

Lay a crepe in the middle of a large plate and spoon on some of the fruit compote across the crepe in the middle. Roll the two ends of the crepe over the line of compote and spoon more fruit over the top of the crepe. Add some soft whipped cream, a chocolate lattice cage and garnish with a sprig of mint. The fruit compote can be either cold or hot depending on the season.

Japanese pumpkin frittata
served with bush tomato chutney

Pumpkin

Commonly known as winter squash, pumpkins are a member of the squash family. There are a wide variety of pumpkins available including butternut, Jarrahdale, Japanese and golden nugget. Each of these can be used in soups, baked, mashed or roasted. Pumpkin seeds are rich in fats and protein and may be roasted and salted as a snack or garnish.

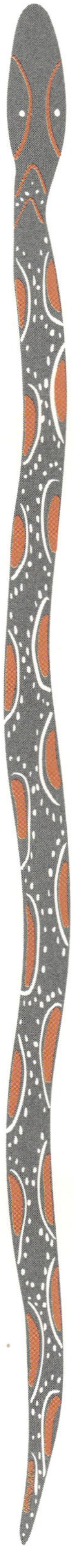

This is one of the few dishes where Vic would agree to using more than one or two of his seasonings but because you eat through the slice of frittata in layers, each mouthful stands alone in flavour - even the pumpkin.
My tip for this dish is to check the pumpkin every 15 minutes and if it starts to crack, turn the oven down because if it springs too many leeks the egg mix will just form an omelette all over the baking tray. Believe me, I've had it happen. ***MM***

serves 8

1 large Japanese pumpkin
3 large zucchini
1 large eggplant
3 large red capsicums
6 eggs
250ml cream
1 bunch wild rocket
8 tablespoon bush tomato chutney
(see page 185)
or use any piquant, slightly sweet relish

½ teaspoon Alpine Pepper
½ teaspoon Wildfire Spice
½ teaspoon Rainforest Rub
½ teaspoon Fruit Spice
½ teaspoon Red Desert Dust
½ teaspoon Oz Lemon

1. rub the pumpkin with oil and sprinkle with salt; place in the oven 180°C for 30-40 minutes
2. while it is cooking slice the vegetables and char grill them until soft, turning often
3. whisk the eggs and add the cream and Alpine pepper
4. scoop the seeds from the pumpkin and season the inside flesh with Fruit Spice – this really brings up the fruity notes of pumpkin and adds a lot to the finished dish
5. begin layering the vegetables using a different spice on each layer - I used Wildfire Spice, Red Desert Dust, Oz Lemon and Rainforest Rub on the layers
6. pour in the egg mixture and place in the oven at 180°C for about 20-30 minutes
7. test if it is cooked by lightly shaking the tray; if the centre doesn't wobble it is ready or you could use the old trick of sticking a skewer in the centre if it comes out clean it's done
8. wash the rocket in cold water and shake dry
9. and get ready to present the dish

The styling is really simple. Just take a look at our picture.

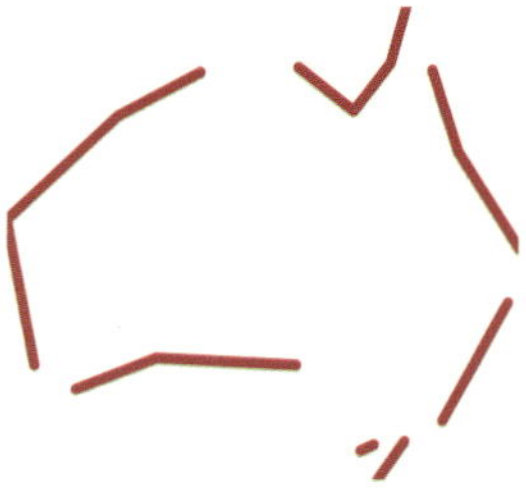

White bean cassoulet

A cassoulet is traditionally a rich, hearty stew of various meats and or beans with a mix of starchy and aromatic vegetables and herbs. Use any root vegetables you can get including parsnips, swedes, yams or even beetroot. You can obviously add other flavourings too but remember, the damper has plenty of complexity of taste. ***BC***

serves 4

Australian olive oil for frying
a tablespoon butter
100g diced carrot
100g diced turnip
100g diced potato
100g diced sweet potato
100g diced Spanish onion
100g diced celery
200g white beans
5-or 6 crushed pepperberries or
½ teaspoon Alpine Pepper
2 litres vegetable stock (page 185)
a generous pinch Outback Salt
Continental parsley

1. In a large pot, drizzle in the olive oil and add the butter and sauté the celery, carrot and onion
2. allow the vegetables to caramelise and season with salt, if desired
3. add the vegetable stock, then the remaining vegetables
4. bring to the boil and simmer for 45 minutes or until the potatoes are soft

Serve in a traditional cassoulet dish with a lid or in individual soup bowls. Garnish with chopped parsley and serve the cassoulet with Riberry and blue cheese damper. (*see page 42*).

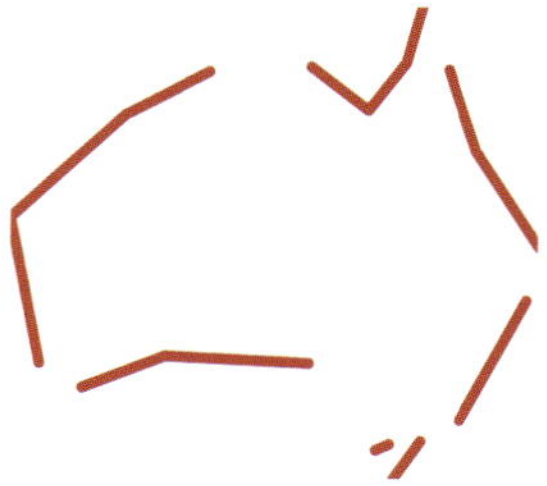

Riberry and blue cheese damper

Damper

Damper was the mainstay of the early settlers in Australia. They used water, bi-carb and coarse flour occasionally 'stretched' with flour milled from wild seeds or nuts. But Aborigines have been cooking this way for tens of thousands of years before them. They took to wheat flour damper readily instead of collecting and milling the far more nutritious wild seeds (it was back-breaking, laborious work).
To cook in, the settlers carried heavy, cast iron camp ovens* whereas the Aborigines had developed quite sophisticated baking methods using nothing more than an open fire, hot coals and the heated ground under the fire.
Do you want to know how? First start by rubbing two sticks together ...

* Cast iron camp ovens also often broke on the rough roads and to address this, a ringer from Bedourie Station developed a much lighter, pressed steel one, now known as a Bedourie oven.

Bedourie oven

The best feature of the camp oven is that to clean it, all you do is burn off any residues and wipe away the dry charcoal. Pack the oven in a Hessian bag, separately wrapping the lid to protect it and the oven is ready to use for next time. ***BC***

serves 8

800g self raising flour
250ml milk (approximately, as this changes with the humidity, so plus or minus 50ml)
a pinch of Outback Salt
50g riberries (glacé riberries are good here)
100g blue cheese

glacé riberries

1. pre-heat the oven (and the camp oven, if you're using one)
2. sift the self raising flour and salt into a bowl
3. add milk to the flour and salt to make a soft dough without over-working the mix, it should be just incorporated and as airy as possible
4. add the riberries and the coarsely broken up blue cheese
5. shape into a round loaf and dust with a little more flour
6. sprinkle a little flour to the camp oven to check the heat and lessen the damper sticking or use a floured, shallow, 25cm round, cake tin if just oven baking
7. bake at 180°C in your conventional oven for 30 to 40 minutes, or until the loaf makes a hollow sound when tapped on the bottom; or if cooking in the camp oven, fit the heated lid and place the camp oven onto hot coals and add more hot coals onto the lid; if there's a wind blowing, build a windbreak or replace the coals regularly and pile up some extra hot coals on the windward side as this will cool off and make the baking un-even; also turn the camp oven often to help distribute the heat

Serve hot or warm, with or without butter and either pull apart into rough chunks for dunking or slice the damper up for sandwiches or toast.

Most Sydneysiders are convinced that this is the best harbour in the world and as for the seafood .....

Sydney Harbour

Recipes from Sydney Harbour

Sydney Sushi

Makes 7-8 medium sized sushi rolls

Sushi Rice

2 cups (450g) sushi rice
2½ cups (625ml) water
100ml Japanese red vinegar or substitute rice vinegar, if necessary
a dash of mirin
40g castor sugar
20g salt
4cm square of kombu seaweed

1. Sushi rice needs "polishing" prior to being cooked; measure the rice and put it into a bowl; pour a generous amount of water over it and stir swiftly, then discard the water; wash again, rubbing the rice and rinsing; repeat this procedure until the water runs clear then drain well in a sieve
2. after polishing the rice, put it in rice cooker with 630ml of water and leave the rice to cook
3. prepare the sushi vinegar; combine half the Japanese red vinegar, mirin, salt, sugar and kombu in a saucepan and heat to dissolve the sugar but do not boil; allow to cool and then add the remaining vinegar (this re-introduces the aromatics); when preparing fish or seafood sushi use less sugar for a lighter flavoured rice
4. once the rice is cooked and while hot, place it a flat-bottomed bowl and pour the sushi vinegar into it and mix it through thoroughly with a wooden spoon or spatula being careful not to mash the rice
5. allow to cool slightly before using in sushi roll

Sushi Rolls

Using nori seaweed, you can make a variety of fillings for your sushi rolls. For ease, keep your hands wet when placing the sushi rice onto the nori sheets, as it prevents the rice from sticking to your hands. You will need a sushi mat for ease of rolling the nori.

Some ideas for fillings include

Oz Lemon with smoked salmon and cucumber
Wildfire spiced tuna and mayonnaise
King prawns with pickled Buderim ginger and Red Desert Dust
Snow pea shoots, cucumber, lettuce, Oz Lemon and mayonnaise

Oysters Outback

freshly shucked Sydney rock oysters
grated cheese, try the available Australian native flavoured cheeses
Red Desert Dust
finely chopped emu prosciutto

Simply top the oysters with the grated cheese and prosciutto, be generous with the Red Desert Dust seasoning and flame using a torch to melt the cheese. Alternatively, put under a grill to do the same.

Wild lime oysters – a classic in simplicity but pure in its delivery

a selection of Sydney rock, Port Stephens, Ceduna, Wallis Lake and Pacific oysters
small desert limes
finger lime 'caviar'
chervil

Cut each desert lime ¾ the way through cutting across the small fruits in order to fan them out over each oyster. Garnish with ¼ teaspoon finger lime 'caviar' and a chervil leaflet.

Desert lime

Australian limes are fruits of several species of indigenous citrus usually found in dry coastal rainforests or outback arid areas.

The most popular native lime is the small but juicy, yellow desert lime (pictured) found in central Queensland.

Juice for beverages, cosmetics and dressings is manufactured from the creek lime.

A newcomer is the finger lime which is gaining attention for its globular vessicles. Called lime caviar it is used as a condiment for a host of fusion cuisine dishes.

Seafood platter

Our choice of seafood in Sydney is only second to the fish markets in Tokyo, so we are very lucky. Our seafood markets are also very accessible. However, choosing farmed or well managed species will keep our choices up by protecting fish stocks from being over-exploited. **BC**

Soused sea perch fillets

Cooking this way can be made even easier for big batches of fish (or scallops, prawns, yabbies etc) if you have a strainer or tray with drainer holes in the bottom to fit into the poaching pan. The idea is to keep the poaching liquid hot and not to cool it off too much each time the cold seafood goes in. Cook one batch, drain and spice it up and then add the next batch to the constantly simmering liquid.

serves 4

4 x 200-250g sea perch fillets (or other white fleshed, not too fishy fish)
300ml water
300mls white wine vinegar
300ml white wine
¼ teaspoon Outback Salt
3-4 desert limes
½ teaspoon Oz Lemon

1. In a shallow, poaching pan combine water, wine and vinegar and bring to a boil
2. add the fish (cut into bite-size pieces) to the boiling stock; it will take about 6-7 minutes to cook so after 2 minutes from adding the fish, turn down the heat to a gentle boil
3. remove the fish and place on paper toweling to absorb the excess moisture
4. dust with the Oz Lemon and season with Outback Salt

Simply serve the finished fish as is with the small limes scattered over it or alternatively, use the Oz Lemon to flavour a mayonnaise or some reduced white balsamic vinegar.

Serve with rice and /or wild rice, couscous, bulgar, barley or other grains (Vic tells me he adds some hijiki seaweed and chicken stock to raw rice, cooks it with the absorption method and then forks through some rice wine vinegar or mirin and palm sugar once it's done – you could even make sushi with this, adding a piece of the fish to the formed rice and cutting each lime into a fan for on top)

Rosella

Wild rosella for culinary use is not the bird but a brilliant red, flower-like fruit case with an acid-crisp taste. The edible portion consists of the petals and sepals of the fertilised flower.

Wild rosella is marketed as a frozen fruit as well as an extract which is easy to use as a flavouring and natural colour agent. It is finding applications in cosmetics, beverages and confectionery.

Sydney Salad

The best part of this salad is the dressing which can be added up to a day ahead and won't turn the lettuces to sludge. In fact, it makes it stay firm and fresh due to osmosis. **VC**

serves 4

For the salad

1. *a goodly amount of mesclun salad mix including rocket, radicchio, coral, coz, cresses, snow pea sprouts and edible petals*
2. *your choice of boiled quail eggs (emu eggs take too long to hard boil and weigh the salad down a bit), fancy tomatoes, avocado slices, pomegranate seeds, riberries or whatever*
3. *proscuitto – try to find emu or roo proscuitto or settle for the common variety if you must*
4. *a handful of croutons (buy them or make them yourself from diced, de-crusted bread slices which can be dried in a low temperature oven with the door open and then tossed in olive oil and melted butter to coat them)*
5. *and the garnish … some witlof and a carrot*

For the dressing

1. *a punnet of strawberries (they don't have to be the best in terms of ripeness)*
2. *½ teaspoon Fruit Spice*
3. *1 teaspoon Alpine pepper (or half this if you want less of a zing)*

1. Prepare the dressing by blending the strawberries to a purée
2. microwave about 3 tablespoons of water in a small bowl or cup until it is quite hot but not boiling and steep the seasonings in it; allow to cool a little and add this mix to the strawberry purée (if the strawberries were chilled you can combine it all together right off)
3. cut the carrot lengthwise carefully and fashion a long spear which you pass through appropriately cut holes in the bases of carefully separated witlof leaves which you arrange to make like the Opera House sails; store this garnish in cold water until you need it

Arrange your salad on a platter and set the garnish in place. Scatter the accompaniments around the salad including the slices of proscuitto and pour on the dressing generously before finishing with the croutons.

Leave these and possibly the garnish as well if you are preparing the salad way ahead of time, although if you carefully plastic wrap the all-but-croutoned salad, it will be fine; just add the croutons prior to serving.

Australian Rainforest Rub

a seasoning developed for Dining Downunder by Vic Cherikoff

A crusting, dusting mix with some wild top notes

Spicemaster notes:

COLOUR - pale yellow mix with bright red chilli fines, sesame seeds and green herb flecks

AROMA - spicy, roasted chicken nose with a sweet lemon, lime and lemongrass oil bouquet

PALATE - full chicken and spice mid-palate with pepper and chilli heat followed by complex herbaceous citrus aromatics and toasted seed

STORAGE - chilled storage recommended

We Aussies love chilli so this herb and spice mix has a bit in it to add those special tingles for your tongue. It's not too hot but formulated to make you sit up and take note and the flavour blends well with the lemon myrtle, lemon aspen and pepperberry in this mix.

I have used a chicken flavoured, vegetarian base for this rub since it is a flavour which goes with a wide range of other foods. However, if you are at all concerned, please note that this is a fully vegetarian seasoning and a great example of the molecular basis of taste where the similarity of the plant protein extract to chicken protein results in the same taste to our brains.

One of my favorite uses for Rainforest Rub is on potato chips. I mean the thin slivers of the humble potato which you buy in a packet as junk food, all deep fried and unhealthy. You might call them crisps. I dust them with Rainforest Rub and the lemony chicken and chilli makes one of the most moreish snacks I know. You might want to try it on the thicker, softer wedges and fries, on corn, sweet potato or taro chips or even on pop corn.

Not surprisingly, Rainforest Rub is great over chicken to intensify the flavour of what must be the world's most popular bird. Use it as a general seasoning in and over practically any meat dish; including roasted, grilled, broiled, barbecued, stir-fried or braised poultry, pork or seafood, veal or game. Sprinkle it over boiled, steamed, baked or stir-fried vegetables or use it in vegetable pies, patties or frittata. Season stews, stocks, soups and sauces and like all of my mixes, you can add it to breads and batters for a savoury twist to these.

As a way to carry the seasoning on foods such as yabbies, crays, lobster, octopus, calamari, prawns or shrimp, mix it with breadcrumbs or a fine polenta. You can even add some grated cheese such as a cheddar or parmesan. Then shallow fry or oven bake, if it's appropriate or else just sprinkle it on and possibly just-melt the cheese under the grill.

Benjamin's background

My initial introduction to native herbs and spices was as an apprentice at the Watermark Restaurant under the guidance of chef, Kenneth Leung. Looking back, Kenneth was amongst the first, well known Australian chefs to incorporate Australian flavours into a fine dining restaurant. We used wattleseed in brulée, fresh rosella in jams and relishes, lemon myrtle in dressings, bunya nuts in salads and akudjura in breads.

From my limited experience at the Watermark, I was inspired to learn more about the native ingredients available and incorporate them into my menu planning. After a little research, it appeared that Vic Cherikoff was the leading authority on native foods. I read his books, read articles and took a course on native ingredients as part of my chef training. What gradually emerged was that there was much more to native cuisine than searing kangaroo fillet and serving it medium rare with a beetroot jam like most chefs were doing at the time (and some still do).

So I set about experimenting while cooking at Great Keppel Island Resort and at the Parkroyal Perth with native fruits, spices and herbs in all types of cooking. I produced dishes and accompaniments like Sydney rock oysters smoked with paperbark, bush tomato and onion chutneys and lemon myrtle chilli sauce, salt & wild pepper prawns to name just a few. I realised that success could be had if the native ingredients were introduced into regular dishes and carefully balanced with typical ingredients.

Chefs across Australia started to incorporate native ingredients into their menus, just as I had, but the trend was still rather restricted to within Australia. So with the popularity of Olympics and the world taking interest in Australia, I formed a company to promote our native ingredients overseas. I cooked at hotels, resorts and clubs right throughout Asia introducing Australian native flavours to diners. Each and every city embraced the new flavours and chefs doing similar Australian promotions in Asia and now, in Europe and the US, still generate the same interest. I believe that this interest is also starting to gather momentum here at home.

I was delighted when my mentor when I was a young chef, Vic Cherikoff, rang me and asked if I would be interested in cooking on his new television series promoting Australian cuisine. Vic said he wanted to create a series which was fun, informative and instructional to viewers and he wanted to show how to use the ingredients correctly and that the flavours are not limited to fine dining restaurant meals.

Now, as Dining Downunder begins to be broadcast around the world, authentically Australian ingredients are becoming more accessible and available to cooks and chefs globally, I would like to thank Vic for inviting me to be involved in the evolution process. I would also like to thank Vic for his continued support and I look forward to turning international cuisine upside down with him soon.

Benjamin Christie

We traveled from Buderim, the ginger capital of Australia to Noosa Beach where ginger was used from entrée through to dessert.

Sunshine Coast

Recipes from Bistro C, Noosa Beach Qld

Thai style whole snapper

Serves 1 - 2

1 whole snapper (approx 600-700g)
20g fresh Australian ginger
50g snow pea sprouts
20g coriander
40g cucumber
40g shallots
40g red capsicum
1 red chilli
black sesame seeds

Dressings
20g Roman basil
20g Thai basil
20g ginger, minced
1 lime, juiced
5g palm sugar
a pinch of salt
10ml light flavoured olive oil (or canola)
1 mango, peeled and de-seeded
100ml mirin
½ teaspoon ginger juice

1. Place the mango flesh in a blender with the mirin and ginger juice and blend to smoothness; strain and transfer to a squeeze bottle for convenience of use
2. as a second dressing, blend the basils, ginger, lime juice, palm sugar, salt and oil to a smooth sauce; strain and transfer to a squeeze bottle for convenience of use
3. slice the ginger and place it in the belly of the fully scaled and cleaned snapper
4. using a thick wooden skewer, skewer the head and tail to hold the fish in a crescent
5. spray the fish with a little canola oil and place in a hot oven at 170°C for approx 20 minutes or until cooked
6. while the fish is cooking, finely slice the cucumber, shallots and capsicum place into a bowl; add the snow pea sprouts and some of the basil dressing
7. toss well and place a mound in the centre of a large plate

To finish the dish, position the 'swimming' snapper on top of the salad. Drizzle criss-crossing lines of the two dressings around the salad and garnish the edges of the plate with finely chopped chilli and black sesame seeds.

King prawn salad with avocado salsa

Serves 1

4 cooked large king prawns
½ avocado
2 shallots
2 sprigs coriander
20g pickled ginger
10ml lime juice

Sauce
garlic
4 roma tomatoes
2 chilli
1 small onion
50g butter
100ml water
5g salt flakes

1. Roughly chop all the ingredients for the sauce
2. in a small pot, sauté the garlic, chilli and onion in the butter; add the chopped tomatoes and water; bring to the boil and then simmer for 60 minutes; allow to cool then blend and strain; season with salt, as needed
3. peel the prawns, leaving the head on and set aside
4. finely chop the pickled ginger, avocado, shallots and coriander; place in a bowl and combine with lime juice

On a plate, place the salsa into a small mould and remove the mould. Place the prawns on top of the salsa carefully twisting the prawn tails together to give a little height to the dish. Use a skewer through the centre of the prawns to secure them and add to the presentation. Around the edge of the salsa, drizzle a little of the tomato chilli sauce.

Ginger poached peaches

Serves 4

4 medium sized peaches
400ml water
400g castor sugar
20g ginger, sliced
½ red chilli
½ lemon grass, coarsely chopped
2 sprigs fresh mint

For the panna cotta
450ml cream
4 tablespoons castor sugar
3 gelatine leaves or 1¼ teaspoons gelatine
5g wattleseed
10ml wattleseed extract

For the panna cotta
1. Heat the cream, wattleseed and sugar over low heat, stirring until it reaches simmering point but do not boil vigorously; stir to dissolve the sugar, continue heating for 3 minutes then remove from heat
2. soak the gelatine leaves in a little cold water until it is fully soft, squeeze the leaves of excess water and stir into the hot cream; if using powdered gelatine, sprinkle it evenly over the surface of the hot cream and leave for a minute or two to absorb moisture then stir into the cream until it dissolves
3. add the wattleseed extract and pour the mixture into 125ml dariole moulds
4. cover tightly with plastic film and refrigerate until set
5. to unmould the panna cotta, dip the moulds into hot water briefly or wrap them in a towel dipped in hot water and tip them out onto shallow serving bowls

For the peaches
1. In a pot, combine the peaches, water, castor sugar, lemon grass, chilli and ginger
2. bring to the boil and simmer for 30 minutes
3. remove the peaches and remove their skins

Serve the peaches in bowls with the panna cotta and some of the syrup. Garnish with a slice of almond bread and fresh mint.

Ginger prawn and noodle salad

Lemon Aspen

Lemon aspen is a rainforest fruit found along the eastern coast of Australia. It has an appealing acid character unlike any conventional citrus and has a fresh menthol and eucalyptus aftertaste.

The juice is very versatile and is a good replacement for lemon juice in most applications. Store the juice in the refrigerator and it will keep for months. The dried fruit pulp is commonly used in seasonings.

The lemon aspen syrup may be the only challenging ingredient in this dish. For a substitute, try a mix of 10ml lemon juice, 80g palm sugar and 70ml (¼ cup) of water. ***BC***

serves 4

Salad
1 packet vermicelli glass noodles (rice or mung bean)
20 green prawns or shrimp, no heads or tails, peeled and de-veined
10ml olive oil
15ml light soy sauce
200g snow peas shoots, chopped
100g bean sprouts
80g snow peas, coarsely chopped
50g macadamia nuts, coarsely chopped
50g shiitake mushrooms, coarsely chopped

Dressing
80ml lemon aspen syrup
15ml white wine vinegar
2 to 6 chillies (depending on their heat and size), de-seeded and finely chopped
1 tablespoon minced ginger
¼ teaspoon Oz Lemon

Salad
1. Place the vermicelli noodles into boil hot water; turn the heat off and allow them to sit for 3 to 4 minutes then strain and cool with cold water
2. marinate the prawns with olive oil and light soy sauce
3. place the prawns on to a hot char-grill for about 3 to 4 minutes, turning once done
4. roast the macadamia nut pieces in a dry pan on the barbecue while constantly tossing them until the fines begin to darken; transfer them to a large mixing bowl to cool

Dressing
1. To the lemon aspen syrup, add enough of the vinegar to lessen the sweetness and give a suggestion of tartness
2. add some of the chopped chilli
3. grate a knuckle of ginger on a slab grater and squeeze a teaspoonful of the juice into the dressing
4. allow the mix to stand for the flavours to infuse

Once the prawns are cooked, combine all of the ingredients, including the dressing in the bowl with the toasted macadamia nuts. Toss well and place onto a large serving plate and dust with Oz Lemon to finish.

Lemon Myrtle

Lemon myrtle leaves are similar in taste to a blend of the oils of lemon grass, lemon and lime with a pleasant sweet character sometimes with a bubblegum note.

The quality of the essential oils in lemon myrtle leaves determines the price with leaf of lesser quality being used in cosmetics, detergents and toiletries.

The leaves are generally used dried or distilled for their 'essence'. Oz Lemon is becoming the preferred source of lemon myrtle for reasons of economy and application (see page 86).

Whole baby salmon
with soy pepper dressing

You can use fillets with the skin on for this if you don't like staring your meal in the eye. You could experiment with the dressing, as there are plenty of possibilities using Australian herbs or seasonings e.g. Oz Lemon, which will add citrus notes to go with the ginger. ***MM***

serves 4

For the dish
4 whole baby salmon, cleaned
1 tablespoon minced ginger
1 bunch of shallots
4 serves (1 punnet) shiitake mushrooms
4 serves snow peas
2 cups bean sprouts
1 teaspoon Rainforest Rub
4 tablespoons pickled ginger
lemon myrtle oil

Soy pepper dressing
100ml low salt soy sauce
80ml mirin
5ml fish sauce
1 tablespoon minced ginger
2 teaspoons Alpine Pepper
a pinch Fruit Spice

For the fish

1. stuff each salmon with the shallots and ginger, preheat oven to 160°C
2. warm a fish pan and rub the salmon with a little oil
3. when the pan is hot seal the salmon on both sides
4. place in the oven for eight minutes
5. remove the fish; test for doneness and brush the top with lemon myrtle oil
6. slice the shiitake mushrooms and de-string the snow peas
7. warm a wok or large pan and stir-fry the three vegetables
8. season with the Rainforest Rub

For the dressing

Warm the mirin in a small saucepan and squeeze in the juice from the ginger. You need about 5ml of juice all up for flavour. Add the Alpine Pepper and Fruit Spice and bring to a gentle simmer. Remove from heat, add fish sauce and soy and it's done.

Place the vegetables in the centre of a large plate and lay the fish on top. Drizzle plenty of dressing around the plate and serve extra in side dishes.

Behind the scenes ...

Milk

CPG

This restaurant breaks all the rules of location, location, location but our Dining Downunder chef, Mark McCluskey cooked up a heap of trade.

Hills District

Chocolate mousse tart
with gumleaf cream and wild rosella flowers

Chocolate really suits some specific Australian flavours. If we think of semi-sweet, dark, rich chocolate, then Australian peppermint, gumleaf oil and aniseed myrtle complement well. Quandong, Kakadu plum, Illawarra plum, wild rosella but particularly Wattleseed really go well with white chocolate.

Then for the middle of the road; milk chocolate, I'd suggest glace riberries, Oz Lemon, some of the spicy flavours and paperbark smoke flavours. Try some of these in this mousse recipe and see what your tastebuds tell you. ***VC***

serves 4

200g plain flour
35g castor sugar
50g butter, softened
2 eggs
2 gelatine leaves
125g chocolate chips
200ml cream
3 drops gumleaf oil
35g castor sugar
4 glazed rosella flowers

1. In a food processor using a pulse action, combine the plain flour, 35g of castor sugar and the softened butter
2. to this mix, add one egg being careful not to over beat; if the pastry is overworked it becomes tough
3. once mixed, wrap the dough in plastic wrap and refrigerate for at least 1 hour; this recipe can be doubled easily and the excess well wrapped in plastic wrap and frozen for other recipes
4. on a well floured bench, quickly roll out the pastry to about 5mm thickness and shape the pastry to fit the desired flat tray, in this case, 4 x 5cm flan tins
5. press the pastry up the sides of the tin; rest the tins in the fridge for a further 20 minutes
6. place a piece of greaseproof paper into the tin and fill with rice; this is known as blind baking and ensures the pastry does not slide down or form bubbles on the base; bake at 160°C for 15 minutes
7. when the cases are cool, place 125ml of cream into a small pot and bring to the boil, then remove from the heat
8. soak the gelatine leaves in cold water
9. place chocolate chips and the remaining egg into a blender and process for 30 seconds
10. while the machine is running, slowly pour the heated cream into the chocolate mixture blend until well mixed and the chocolate chips are melted, then add the squeezed gelatine
11. pour the mix into cool tart cases and refrigerate until set
12. with the remaining 75ml cream, briskly whisk together with 15g sugar and gum leaf oil; taste the cream after 2 drops of gumleaf oil adding more if necessary

Serve garnished with a dollop of sweetened gumleaf cream and glacé rosella flowers and syrup.

We visited
VAT 107 in
the heart of
Margaret
River
Township for
some local
specialities.

Margaret River

Recipes from VAT 107, Margaret River WA

Flame grilled Western Australian marron with a Greek salad and oregano dressing

Serves 4

6 x 400g marron
16 black Kalamata olives
3 Roma tomatoes
1 small cucumber
130g fetta cheese
1 small Spanish onion
½ bunch oregano
500ml olive oil
3 lemons
20g sea salt

1. Nowadays marron is primarily sold live, so when you buy them, place them in the freezer for about 3 hours; after this, cut them in half down their length
2. start by heating the BBQ, so it will be ready by the time you have prepared the Greek salad and oregano dressing
3. in a mortar and pestle or food processor, crush the oregano leaves with a little salt; continue crushing to form a fine paste, then add the olive oil and the juice from 1 lemon; transfer to a sauce bottle for serving
4. to prepare the salad; simply slice the cucumber, Roma tomato and Spanish onions and place into a bowl with the Kalamata olives; cut the fetta cheese into small cubes and add to the salad; finish by adding a little oregano dressing to the salad
5. once the BBQ is hot, simply grill the marron; start with the flesh side down on the BBQ for about 3 minutes; turn over and finish with the shell side down; check for doneness by looking at the texture or by inserting a metal skewer through the thickest part of the flesh for 3~5 seconds, removing it and carefully testing the temperature by touching the part of the skewer at the middle of the marron meat against your lower lip; if it is warm to hot, it's cooked
6. place a small amount of the Greek salad onto the plate, then top with 3 half tails per person.
7. finish the marron with a little oregano dressing and serve each dish with half a lemon on the side.

Tempura oysters with sweet soy dipping sauce

Serves 4

2 dozen shucked oysters
1 egg
250ml chilled water
2 kg ice
100g flour
1litre vegetable oil
30ml mirin
30ml sake
50ml sweet soy sauce
20ml light soy sauce
10g ginger, minced

1. In a large pot, heat the vegetable oil to about 180~190°C
2. in a small bowl combine the mirin, sake, sweet soy sauce, light soy sauce and ginger; whisk and allow to stand
3. in another bowl combine the egg and the water; whisk well.
4. slowly fold in the flour, taking care not to over mix the batter; stand the batter bowl in another bowl of ice to keep it chilled
5. carefully remove each oyster from its shell, set the shell aside
6. test the vegetable oil, by placing a little bread in the oil; if it starts bubbling, then it's hot enough
7. batter each oyster in the tempura and fry till golden brown; remove and drain on paper towelling
8. place each oyster back into their shell and serve with a small dish of the dipping sauce

Szechwan twice cooked duck with Chinese pancakes

Serves 4

1 Size 17 duck
3 star anise
5g Szechwan peppercorns
1 cinnamon stick
60g salt
50g ginger, minced
½ bunch coriander
20ml soy sauce
30g corn flour
1 litre vegetable oil
1 cucumber
3 shallots
100ml Hoisin sauce
5ml sesame oil
4 tablespoons sweet chilli sauce (thinned, if necessary with mirin)
4 or 5 Chinese pancakes per serve

1. Start by heating a wok, then add the star anise, peppercorns, and cinnamon stick and toast till just smoking; remove and allow to cool
2. in a spice blender or mill, grind and combine with salt
3. take half of the ground salt and pepper mix and rub into the duck's skin and put a little in the cavity of the duck
4. roughly cut the coriander, add the ginger and place in the cavity also; place in the fridge for 5 hours uncovered, which allows the skin to dry out a little
5. the first cooking process is to steam the duck; if you do not have a steamer, partly fill a deep pot with boiling water and place a rack in it, just above the water line and heat at a constant simmer
6. place the whole duck on the rack breast side down and steam for about 70 minutes, topping up the boiling water as needed
7. remove and allow to cool, brush the duck occasionally with soy sauce
8. when finally cool, cut the duck into 4 portions
9. cut the shallots and cucumber in to 7cm lengths
10. with the Hoisin sauce, whisk in the sesame oil
11. combine the remaining salt and pepper mix with corn flour
12. in a wok, heat the vegetable oil to about 180~190°C; test the oil, by placing a little bread in it and if it starts by bubbling, then the oil is hot enough
13. dust each portion of duck with the salt and pepper mix, then deep fry till golden brown in colour
14. serve with just steamed Chinese pancakes, Hoisin sauce, shallots and cucumber and sweet chilli sauce

Chinese pancakes (Hong Kong or Peking style)

Makes approx 25 pancakes

600g plain flour
75g glutinous flour
270ml hot water
½ teaspoon salt
a drizzle of sesame oil

1. combine the dry ingredients into a bowl; make a well in the centre and add the hot water, stirring rapidly with a wooden spoon
2. knead the dough well on a lightly floured surface until it is smooth and firm
3. return the dough to the mixing bowl; cover and leave to stand for 1 hour
4. pull the dough apart to make about 25 equal sized pieces
5. roll out each piece to form a 15cm pancake; brush the top with sesame oil
6. heat a skillet and brush the bottom with sesame oil; then fry each pancake for about 30 seconds on each side
7. stack the pancakes on a plate and allow to cool

Just prior to serving, place the pancakes into a bamboo basket and steam for 10 minutes or place in a microwave oven along with a shallow bowl with a tablespoonful of water. Microwave on high for 30~60 seconds.

Salt and pepper yabbies

Marron

Marron are very large freshwater crayfish native to the permanent rivers in the forested, high rainfall areas in the south west of Western Australia.

Marron is a traditional Aboriginal word for the crustacean in the language of the local people in the area.

It is only coincidence that the word 'Marron' is also the French word for water chestnuts and a comparison can be made with the colour, shape and taste of the tail to that of water chestnuts.

On average marron grow to around 150g - 300g weight, but have been known to grow up 2kg.

Late at night down in Chinatown, many restaurants serve up this treat using either fresh prawns or squid in their own unique salt and Szechwan pepper blends. I thought yabbies would bring sweetness to the dish giving it a further dimension.
Nowadays, most fish shops and seafood markets in Australia have live yabbies available or you can catch your own in farm dams and most of our larger inland rivers. Try this recipe with chicken strips as well. ***BC***

serves 4

20 yabbies (prawns, shrimp or squid)
100g rice flour or breadcrumb
5g salt
10g Alpine Pepper
80g rocket (arugula) or mizuna leaves
2-3 litres vegetable oil
skewers

1. Start out by freezing your catch for 2 hours immediately before the preparation
2. begin by heating up vegetable oil in a deep pot on the stove. Take a lot of care when deep frying and watch the protruding handle on some pots since bumping it can splash the oil and lead to a fire. I like to use vegetable or peanut oil as the plain flavours don't over-power the subtle flavours of the seafood. (Vic tells me that they also have a higher smoke point than olive or other nut oils so you reduce the oxidation of the fats and this makes them better for deep frying.)
3. remove the head from each yabby and peel off the shell by snipping the edges of the shells with kitchen scissors. You can reserve the shells and heads, roast them and make a delicious stock or bisque (not needed for this recipe) so freeze everything but the tail meat for up to a few weeks until you need it
4. depending on the size of each yabbie, you may need 5 to 6 smaller tails per skewer or 2 to 3 larger ones. Mix the salt & pepper with the rice flour and coat the skewered yabbies generously
5. before you cook the yabbies, you'll need to test the heat of the oil. As we demonstrated on the show, you can do this by placing a skewer in the heated oil. If bubbles come out of the end of the skewer, the oil is hot enough. Lower the yabbies into the hot oil, they will need only 2-3 minutes to cook and the coating should be golden brown. Drain on paper toweling to soak up any excess oil
6. Arrange the skewers as shown or simply stack them and serve with a small salad.

Another version of this recipe is to poach the un-seasoned yabbies on skewers in seafood or chicken stock and serve them with a sweet and sour lemon aspen dressing (see Master recipes page 184).

Enoki

Sometimes referred to as Enokitake, the enoki mushroom is a white, Japanese variety with a mild flavour yet delicate flavour. They have a long, 10cm stem with a tiny, very white cap. They are available all year round and are used in salads for their crunchy texture or as a garnish. They are available fresh, picked in the clumps as they grow.

Paperbark smoked duck
with an Illawarra plum sauce

A short cut in this recipe could be to buy Peking duck and briefly smoke it a camp oven lined with paperbark. ***MM***

serves 4

For the dish
4 x 150g duck breast
1 bunch watercress
1chopped chilli hot
4 serves shiitake mushrooms
4 serves enoki mushrooms
1 roll paperbark
1 teaspoon Alpine Pepper

For the sauce
30g Illawarra plums, chopped
20g de-seeded, dark conventional plums, tinned is fine
30ml red wine vinegar
30ml reasonable quality, red wine
1 tablespoon palm sugar
150ml chicken stock
¼ teaspoon Alpine Pepper
¼ teaspoon Fruit Spice

For the sauce

Important note: avoid aluminium cookware when preparing sauces and particularly with Illawarra plums as they will make the sauce astringent and bitter and totally inedible

1. This sauce can be based on a reduction of the meat juices left over from cooking meat such as chicken or beef
2. simply deglaze the pan or oven tray while it's still hot (having removed the cooked meat) with the vinegar; follow with the wine and stock (this is optional if there is enough meat juices in the pan to start); reduce the mixture to about half its volume
3. meanwhile, blend the plums to smoothness and add to the reduction; add the sugar to balance the tartness, increasing the amount if necessary; season with Alpine Pepper and Fruit Spice and keep warm until ready to use

For the dish

1. Use a cast iron or camp oven, line it with damp paperbark (Vic tells me he saves the off-cuts when thinning sheets for this) and set over a medium heat with the lid on
2. crust the duck breast with Alpine Pepper
3. when the camp oven has heated enough to fill with smoke, place the duck breast inside for about 15~20 minutes or until the juices just run clear when the breast is pricked with a skewer
4. remove from the camp oven and rest in a warm place for 5 minutes
5. slice the duck into thin slices
6. slice shitake mushrooms and tease apart the enoki
7. wash the watercress

Place the watercress in the centre of the plate and alternately, layer the mushrooms and duck. Garnish with the chilli and enoki mushrooms or some deep-fried vermicelli. Finish with the Illawarra plum sauce and serve with extra sauce to the side.

Sandpaper figs

Figs are interesting in that they are not true fruits but fleshy receptacles containing dozens of tiny flowers. They often contain tiny wasps which pollinate them and are essential for the receptacle to ripen fully.

Figs are part of the mulberry family. The common, commercialised fig is a native of the Middle East although there are many wild species also found in Australia.

Wild figs such as the Australian coastal sandpaper fig (pictured) and the outback rock fig are probably the only two native varieties with any commercial potential.

Lemony ricotta figs

with grape nectar and macadamia nuts

This is a really simple but delicious dessert which can be substituted any number of ways;

1. Use different fruits such as mango, apricots, peaches or stewed pears
2. use different herbs Australian mint, peppermint or aniseed myrtle
3. mix them into a range of cheeses such as quark or cottage cheese, cream cheeses such as Philadelphia, Neufchatel, mascarpone or even straight sour cream or yoghurt
4. try a range of pure honeys, maple syrup, palm sugar syrup, brandy butter, golden syrup or fruit syrups (rose hip, pomegranate etc);
5. finally, introduce different nuts such as pecans, pistachio, Brazil nuts, pine nuts ***VC***

serves 1

1 large or 2 small figs per serve
1 tablespoon ricotta cheese per fig
¼ teaspoon Oz Lemon
2 tablespoons grape nectar
macadamia nut pieces (toasted) for garnish

Trim the fat end of each fig so that the fruit stands up-right. Cut the thin end with a cross to open up the figs but still keeping them in one piece. Mix the Oz Lemon into the ricotta, preferably at least 2 hours before serving as this allows the flavours to really penetrate the cheese.

Place a tablespoonful of the prepared cheese in each cross cut fig. Grill until the fig is warm and the cheese just bubbles. Plate up the fig, drizzle with the grape nectar and garnish with the toasted macadamia nut pieces. Serve immediately with a strong coffee.

Australian Wildfire Spice ~ a seasoning developed for Dining Downunder by Vic Cherikoff

What I call "Pizza in a Bottle"

Spicemaster notes:

COLOUR - coarse, multi-ingredient, multi-coloured herb, spice and salt flecks

AROMA - complex, mixed spice nose tending to Mediterranean but with a wild woody Australian character and suggestion of pizza

PALATE - full chicken and spice mid-palate with pepper and chilli heat followed by complex herbaceous citrus aromatics and toasted seed

STORAGE - chilled storage recommended

This is my all-purpose, spice mix which includes a bit of zing from Australian mountain pepper combined with a herb finish from the blend of lemon aspen, lemon myrtle and aniseed myrtle. I also include a mob of conventional herbs and spices including paprika, pepper, rosemary, marjoram, parsley, oregano and nutmeg. There's a little garlic and onion for those background flavours and yes, a touch of salt and sugar to finish.

Australian Wildfire Spice is not too spicy but it is a complex flavoring and ideal for barbequing, grilling and baking.

Use it as a dry marinade or rub over seafood, meats, eggs or vegetables.

I add a heaped teaspoonful when baking bread in a bread machine or by hand or for pizza base, crepes or savoury pancakes use the same amount per 500g (about a pound) of dough or batter.

Use Wildfire Spice in burgers, meatloaf or other savoury mince meat or sprinkle some liberally over your next stir-fry, salad, pasta or pizza.

You can also add a sprinkle and infuse the flavour into red wine or mushroom sauces for steaks and chops; add some to warmed olive oil for that tasty dipping oil with some fresh bread or make salad dressings with oil and vinegar and Wildfire Spice to taste.

See what I mean about all-purpose?

I also like mixing some into sour cream and topping baked potatoes or seasoning kumara chips or slices baked in the oven. It turns boring steamed vegetables into something interesting (OK, so you still need a nob of butter as well).

Get some seed mix such as linseeds, sunflower and sesame seeds and maybe some finely chopped almonds and add a generous amount of Australian Wildfire Spice to make a delicious dukkah or spiced seed mix. This can be used as a dip for olive oil soaked bread or as a crusting over meats and seafood for frying, broiling or grilling.

The more you use my Wildfire Spice, the more favourite applications you'll find.

I like to suggest substitutes in case you want to try the recipe but not get the seasoning but there really isn't much like this mix because of the 'bushy-ness' and zing of the mountain pepper, the aromatic citrus of the lemon myrtle, the eucalyptus hint from the lemon aspen and the liquorice notes from the aniseed myrtle. This makes it a hard combination to duplicate.

Australian Red Desert Dust ~ a seasoning developed for Dining Downunder by Vic Cherikoff

A piquant, spicy blend for meats, seafood, egg dishes and vegetables

Spicemaster notes:

COLOUR - Central Australian red sand colour with green, purple-black and bright red flecks and pale tan sesame seeds

AROMA - spicy, peppery primaries with roasted chicken notes and a herb finish

PALATE - initial sweet and salt, followed by a full chicken and pepper mid-palate with complex spice and toasted seed

STORAGE - chilled storage recommended

This is a gutsy, aromatic mix of conventional and native Australian ingredients and ideal as a finishing flavour over meats, potatoes, eggs or cheeses such as baked ricotta. Try a simple grilled cheese on toast sprinkled with Red Desert Dust and taste the added dimensions of the impact from the native Australian ingredients.

Put it on salmon, white or red meats and bake to doneness then blacken the spice mix under the grill or broiler. This lessens the herb notes but brings out the peppery zing and smokey spice flavours.

Red Desert Dust is also a great flavouring for pastry, especially for home made Aussie meat pies but try it in pasta and pizza dough, bread crumbs and batters. It can even be added to bread mixes you might make by hand or in a bread machine. Add about 2 ~ 3% of the flour weight or 3 ~ 4 teaspoonfuls per 500g

There are a few herb inclusions in Red Desert Dust which work as flavour enhancers for tomato dishes such as gumbo, stews or your favourite pasta sauce so add some early in the cooking and let the ingredients combine and meld to a richness you won't forget.
Red Desert Dust can also be used as a dry rub or marinade, adding complexity to meats. Alternatively, mix some into butter or your favourite substitute and melt over cooked meats allowing the warmth to heighten the impact of the ingredients.

Another use is as a general flavouring in dressings, mayonnaise or oil and whisking will help infuse the flavours or warming works, either way, as appropriate. Try adding Red Desert Dust to pancake batter for an interesting savoury crepe which can be filled with tinned tuna, salmon, roast chicken strips etc and moisten with snow pea sprouts or some enoki mushrooms for a simple snack or entrée.

One easy nibbly I often make is to slice Lebanese flat bread into segments, drizzle them generously with olive oil (Australian, of course) and sprinkle on the Red Desert Dust (or try my other seasoning mixes for variety). I might add a little extra salt to some. Lay the segments out on a baking tray and place into an oven at 100°C (212°F) and leave the oven door open a little to help the flatbread dry to crispness. It only takes about 5 minutes. Serve with an Australian riesling, an unwooded chardonnay or an ice cold beer.

This town is changing from a working steel mill harbour to a trendy area to wine and dine. Executive Chef, Nick Flynn shows us how....

Newcastle Harbour

Recipes from the Crowne Plaza Newcastle, NSW

Laksa lemak ayam (chicken with noodles in spiced coconut soup)

Serves 1

100g Hokkien noodles
1 sprig laksa leaves or Vietnamese mint
½ stalk of lemongrass, trimmed and bashed
2 tofu squares, sliced thinly
120g chicken breast
2g salt
3g sugar
100ml coconut milk
2 cups chicken stock
5g tamarind paste
2g chili paste
10g shallots
20g fresh galangal
20g fresh tumeric root
40g fresh bean sprouts
1 kaffir lime leaf
20g fresh coriander

1. Blend galangal, turmeric root, chilli paste and shallots into a paste, add a little water if needed
2. in a small pot, heat vegetable oil, add the blended ingredients, fry until the spices emit a toasty aroma
3. add coconut milk, chicken stock, lemongrass stalks, sugar, salt to taste, tamarind paste and kaffir lime leaf
4. bring to the boil and simmer for 30 minutes
5. slice the chicken breast thinly and place in the pot; cook for 2 minutes and remove pot from heat

In a deep bowl, place in the noodles and cover with laksa soup including chicken breast. Add tofu, bean sprouts and garnish with fresh coriander.

Lemon aspen crème caramel with rosella compote

Serves 8

50ml lemon aspen syrup
200g of white sugar
100ml of water
30ml extra water for dipping pastry brush
1 litre of milk
100g castor sugar
6 large eggs
1 teaspoon of vanilla essence
100g rosella
100g apples
30g raw sugar
1 teaspoon Fruit Spice

1. Preheat the oven to 160°C, while you are preparing the caramel
2. grease eight ovenproof dariole moulds or ramekins which hold around half a cup of liquid
3. in a medium sized saucepan combine the lemon aspen, 100g sugar and 100ml of water over a low heat and bring to the boil; it is important not to stir the caramel to prevent it forming crystals
4. boil for around 5 to 10 minutes brushing any sugar that lands on the side of the saucepan and crystallizes back down into the mixture with a pastry brush dipped in water
5. remove the mixture from the heat when it has changed to a golden caramel or light amber colour; a dark amber colour indicates the caramel is over-cooked and will taste burnt and bitter
6. pour a little of the hot caramel into each of the prepared moulds and swirl the mixture around to cover the bottom of each mould
7. once the caramel is done, in a medium saucepan warm the milk and briefly remove it from the heat
8. in a large bowl, whisk the eggs and 100g castor sugar together until the sugar has nearly dissolved; add the vanilla and warm milk
9. sieve the custard mixture into a jug or pitcher, then skim off any bubbles or froth from the custard; pour evenly into the 8 moulds and place in a baking dish
10. pour hot water (not boiling) into the baking dish until the water reaches half way up the sides of the moulds
11. bake for 30 to 40 minutes until the custard is set; cool and refrigerate for at least 3 to 4 hours before serving

For the compote

1. While the custards are cooling, peel the Granny Smith apples and dice them; squeeze a little lemon juice on the peeled fruit to reduce it browning
2. combine the apples and rosella in a small pot with raw sugar and bring to the boil and simmer
3. once cooked through, remove, add the Fruit Spice and allow the compote to cool; blend if required

To serve, turn the custards out of each mould by holding the mould upside down and pressing your fingers against the edge of the custard. The custard should loosen and slip out onto the serving dish. If necessary shake the mould gently or if all else fails use a hot wet knife around the edge. Pour any caramel liquid left in the moulds over the custard. Serve with rosella compote on the side.

Nick Flynn, Executive Chef

Seafood Laksa

with wild limes and lemon myrtle linguini

In my early days as a chef, I spent some time in South East Asia exploring the different tastes and cuisines of the region. One region which I particularly enjoyed was Georgetown, Penang, the home of the world famous laksa. I learnt their standard recipe from a well known, local chef, who, let me tell you, loves his Laksa super-spicy.
I have adapted his recipe here and added in a native twist to have the taste buds going wild. From time to time, I also add straw mushrooms, English spinach or baby beetroot leaves, snow peas, asparagus or even zucchini. It's also great with chicken breast strips or deep-fried tofu instead of the seafood. ***BC***

serves 4

4 cloves garlic, peeled
50g minced ginger
4 shallots
4 small red chillies (or as hot as you choose)
1 teaspoon peanut oil for frying
1 teaspoon of shrimp paste
500ml coconut milk or 300ml coconut cream
300ml chicken stock
400g snapper fillets cut into 8 pieces
8 - 12 scallops in the half shell
8 king prawns
2 squid tubes
½ teaspoon Oz Lemon
8 Australian desert limes or 8 slices of ordinary limes and a 4 Kaffir lime leaves
60ml lemon aspen syrup
300g lemon myrtle linguini
a generous tablespoon of salt
a dash of sesame seed oil

1. Mince the garlic, ginger, shallots and chilli together using a sharp knife and a levered chopping action; then, in a hot pot with a little oil, quickly fry the minced ingredients allowing the aromatics to be released; add in the shrimp paste and continue frying for half a minute longer
2. add the chicken stock, boil and begin reducing, after a few minutes add the coconut milk, lower the heat a little (keeping at a simmer) and continue reducing, the aim is to reduce the volume to a thick soupy consistency – if you are in a hurry, use coconut cream and you won't have to reduce it so much
3. in another pot, boil some salted water for the lemon myrtle linguini, put in the pasta and make sure it doesn't stick together by gently stirring once the pasta has softened (about 2 minutes) - stirring before this time tends to break the pasta up as it can still be hard and brittle on the inside
4. while the flavour base in the pot is reducing down to around ¼ of its original volume, begin to prepare the seafood; peel and de-vein the de-headed prawns (I keep prawn heads and freeze them until I have the time to roast them and then cook them down in seasoned water to make a rich shell-fish stock which I also freeze in ice cube trays for later use), cut the squid tubes into bite sized pieces and score these with diagonal, parallel cross cuts; finally, remove any bones from the snapper fillets.
5. when the lemon myrtle linguini is cooked, drain it, add a dash of sesame seed oil to stop it sticking (and for flavour, of course) and set aside
6. add the squid, snapper, prawns and finally the scallops, wild limes and lemon aspen syrup to the coconut stock reduction and keep the laksa at a gentle boil until the seafood is cooked

Place a little lemon myrtle linguini into either a bowl, then spoon out the seafood, fishing for 2 pieces of the seafood and two wild limes per serve. Ladle in the laksa sauce, sprinkle on the extra flavour with a little Oz Lemon and top the lot with a sprig of coriander and chervil.

Bugs

Most people are unaware (and probably don't care) that there are two types of bugs in Australia: The Balmain bug (or shovel-nosed sand lobster) and the Moreton Bay bug.

The two distinct differences are that the Balmain bug has its eyes in the centre of the head and the Moreton bay bugs have their eyes on the outer edge. Both have a sweet and succulent flavour, characteristic of most crayfish or lobsters.

When boiled in salted water, the bugs turn a bright orange and are generally served cut straight down the centre, which allows easy access to the white flesh in the tail.

Aussie burger and chips

Add things like melted cheese, fried eggs and chopped chilli. To go a bit more Mediterranean; add a little mint to the lamb, use thin and crispy proscuitto, toast Turkish bread and spread it with bush tomato chutney, then add crispy, fried or baked haloumi cheese. ***MM***

serves 4

6 Desiree potatoes
1 bunch baby beetroots
1kg lamb mince
1 teaspoon Wildfire Spice
1 teaspoon Alpine Pepper
2 egg yolks
¼ cup flour
oil for frying
2 Spanish onions, finely sliced
2 teaspoons sugar
a generous pinch of Outback Salt
¼ bottle of beer (optional) or some water
1 loaf wattleseed and walnut bread (see page 132)
150g bacon or proscuitto
1 fresh pineapple, peeled and thinly sliced (2 slices per serve)
2 sweet vine ripened tomatoes
shredded lettuce of your choice
100ml Alpine Pepper BBQ sauce (see master recipes)

1. Combine the salt and sugar
2. in a deep tray, spread about a third of the mix, place the fillets on top and pack with the remaining cure mix
3. leave for 2 hours at room temperature or chill for 24 hours
4. when the barramundi flesh has firmed up and lightened in colour, rinse in fresh water, drain and dry with paper towels
5. slice into thin pieces cutting across the fillets at an angle of 30°
6. prepare the pasta in salted boiling water for 11 minutes or until al denté, drain and add a dash of olive oil (Australian, of course)
7. top and tail the snow peas removing the string from the edges
8. blanch the snow peas and warrigal greens and refresh in iced water then drain
9. slice the capsicums into thin strips
10. heat up a wok add a little oil and a nob of butter, toss the pasta until golden then add the snow peas, greens and capsicums, dish up the 4 serves
11. to the hot pan, add the barralax slices, toss for about 1 minute; sprinkle with Oz Lemon and serve on top of the pasta

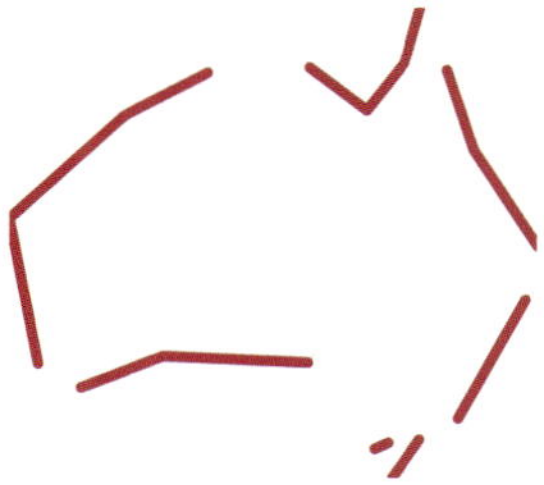

Polenta and Lemon Aspen cake
with sugar bag cream and sugared rosella

We seem to forget that polenta or corn was once only food for native American Indians and is now a world food crop. Contrast this to Australia where the only global food species native to this country is the macadamia nut. But times they are a-changing. VC

serves 4

250g polenta
800ml of water
150ml lemon aspen syrup
2 fresh figs
10 rosella flowers
50g castor sugar
30ml sugarbag
100ml fresh cream
40g glacé riberries

1. In a pot, combine the water, lemon aspen syrup and polenta; bring to the boil, stirring constantly
2. the polenta will take 5 -7 minutes to cook through, once at a boil
3. spoon out the polenta from the pot and place into a flat tray and allow to cool
4. once cool, cut into triangle or hexagon shapes, with three pieces per serve
5. in a bowl, briskly whip the fresh cream to stiff peaks and flavour with the sugarbag; use maple syrup as a substitute; set aside
6. slice the figs into thin slices
7. in another pot, heat castor sugar until dissolved; it may require a little water to soften the mix
8. dip the rosella flowers in to the sugar mix and allow to cool on a plate

Finally assemble the dish, by placing a piece of the polenta on the plate. Then add a little cream and fig slice and repeat, building up the dish. Garnish with cream, riberries and the sugared rosella.

Aussie Slang

We thought we would include this dictionary to accompany the show and the book on thier overseas travels

Barbie : barbecue or BBQ
Bikkie : biscuit also "it cost big bikkies" - it was expensive
Billy : large tin can used to boil water over a campfire for tea
Butchers chook : have a look
Brekkie : breakfast
Chewie : chewing gum
Chokkie : chocolate
Chook : a chicken or an old lady
Coldie : a beer, tinnie
Cut lunch : sandwiches
Damper : bread made from flour and water
Dead dingo's donger, as dry as a : dry
Dead horse : Tomato sauce
Dog's eye : meat pie
Dunny : Toilet or loo outside
Fair dinkum : true, genuine
Fairy floss : candy floss, cotton candy
Fair go : a chance ("give a bloke a fair go")
Fisho : fishmonger
Flake : shark's flesh (sold in fish & chips shops)
G'Day : hello
Grog : liquor, beer ("bring your own grog, you bludger")
Grouse: great, terrific, very good
Jackaroo : a male station hand (a station is a ranch or large grazing property)
Jillaroo : a female station hand
Joey : baby kangaroo
Journo : journalist
Jumbuck : sheep or lamb
Lollies : sweets, candy
Longneck : 750ml bottle of beer in South Australia
Middy : 285 ml beer glass in New South Wales
Milk bar : corner shop that sells takeaway food
Milko : milkman
Mozzie : mosquito
Pav : Pavlova - a rich, creamy Australian dessert

Pig's arse! : I don't agree with you
Piker : Someone who doesn't want to fit in with others socially, leaves parties early
Plonk : cheap wine
Ripper : great, fantastic - "it was a ripper party"
Roo : kangaroo
Sanger : a sandwich
Seven Course Meal : Pie and a six pack
Six Pack : Six beers
Sticky beak : somebody who doesn't mind their own business
Stubby: a 375 ml beer opposite to long neck.
Struth : utter amazement
Truckie : truck driver
True blue : patriotic
Tucker : food
Tucker-bag : food bag
VB : Victoria Bitter Beer
Vegies : vegetables
Vee dub : Volkswagen
Veg out : relax in front of the TV (like a vegetable)
Vejo : vegetarian

REDgum

The historic Boronia House in Mosman is home to Uli and Sean's Redgum Restaurant, recently moved from Manly and here's why their regulars followed them....

Sydney's Northshore

Kumara

Commonly known as orange sweet potato, it was brought to New Zealand by early Maori settlers from its Pacific Island source. The kumara is a large tuberous vegetable which can weigh up to 1kg.

It is not botanically related to the potato but more to Morning Glory (the plant rich in psychoactive alkaloids related to the semi-synthetic hallucinogen, LSD).

Kumara is available in red, gold or orange varieties, each with a deliciously different colour and taste. Kumara is often served roasted, deep fried, mashed or used in casseroles, pies and curries.

Saltbush lamb
with kumara smash

Saltbush lamb has a unique taste quality resulting from the native saltbush on which the animals feed. It is not so much salty as robust, almost rich and yet delicate enough to carry some good spice mixes. ***MM***

serves 4

4 saltbush lamb backstraps on the bone
2 large kumara
oil for frying
a pinch of Fruit spice
several generous pinches Wild thyme mix
a couple of pinches of Alpine Pepper
2 bunches broccolini
200ml lamb jus
4 figs
beetroot jam (see page 80)

1. Remove the meat from the bone with a sharp, boning knife
2. season the lamb with wild thyme and tie it in place, back on the bone
3. pan sear the lamb to brown and cook it in a preheated oven for 8 minutes at 250°C
4. remove the meat from the oven and rest for 8 minutes
5. peel the sweet potatoes and dice, steam in the microwave for about 10 minutes or until soft
6. using the same pan in which the lamb was cooked, add the sweet potato and a drizzle of olive oil and fry until the potato becomes crispy; add Fruit Spice and Alpine Pepper to taste
7. steam the broccolini and grill the figs
8. heat the jus and add a couple of pinches of Alpine Pepper

To serve, remove the lamb from the bone and slice the backstrap. Use a mould to shape the sweet potato, place the broccolini on top and arrange the lamb on top or next to the broccolini and figs. Finish the dish with a little jus and beetroot jam; you won't need much as the lamb is nice and juicy.

Panfried monkfish
with bunya nut hash, rocket and macadamia nut pesto

Macadamia

Many people assume that the macadamia is from Hawaii because of effective marketing by the American producers there. However, they are native to the rainforests of south eastern Queensland and northern New South Wales.

The macadamia was introduced into Hawaii about 1881 where it was initially used as an ornamental and for reforestation. The first Hawaiian plantation dates back to around 1890 while their were commercial planting of macadamias in Australian as early as 1864.

The macadamia nut has a subtle nutty flavour and unique smooth but crunchy texture. It is a creamy white kernel that is very high in mono-unsaturated oils making up around 70% of its composition.

While I was an apprentice chef at the Watermark restaurant in Sydney, the kitchen brigade took turns on who would create the fish of the day offering. You could always tell the best ones as they often sold out by the middle of service and I'm proud of some of the best-selling dishes I concocted during my time there.

Since then, in each restaurant I have run I have showcased the fantastic fish available in Australia, including my favorite coral trout. Although this dish is not one of the specials we created, it is rather similar in presentation and style to those we prepared many years ago. ***BC***

serves 4

400g potatoes
12-18 bunya nuts
4 x 250g monkfish fillets
100g rocket
80g macadamia nuts
50g parsley
100ml olive oil
20g butter
30g honey
¼ teaspoon Outback Salt
½ teaspoon Rainforest Rub
Sprig of watercress for garnish

1. First, peel the potatoes and bring them to the boil in small pot; in another pot, boil the bunya nuts and allow to cool in the boiled water
2. for the pesto; finely chop the macadamia nuts, rocket, parsley or blend together in a food processor and then reduce this mixture to a paste in a mortar and pestle adding a little olive oil, honey, Rainforest Rub and salt to taste.
3. remove the shells from the bunya nuts and chop the nut meat finely; drain the potatoes; coarsely mash both of these in a bowl and season with Outback salt and form into hash brown sized patties
4. in a sauce pan, heat a little olive oil and melt in some butter; panfry the bunya nut hash browns until golden; it may require a little more olive oil during the process; make sure to keep the temperature down to low to avoid any smoking of the oil
5. ensure the fish is free of all bones and in another sauce pan heat a little olive oil and butter and pan fry the monkfish until also golden brown on medium heat

When cooked, place a bunya nut hash brown on the plate, top with the monk fish, then simply garnish with the rocket and macadamia nut pesto and a sprig of watercress.

Coconut and Oz Lemon brulée

serves 6

500ml full cream
130g sugar
3 egg yolks
1 tablespoon coconut milk powder or alternatively, replace 100ml of the cream with coconut cream
½ teaspoon Oz Lemon
2 ripe bananas
sugar

1. Add the coconut powder to the cream and slightly warm the full cream in a pot on the stove
2. place the egg yolks with the sugar in a bowl and whisk briskly, creaming the mixture
3. add the cream to the mixture and add the Oz Lemon
4. place in moulds and place into a deep tray and half fill with warm water half way up the sides of the moulds; cover entire tray with foil; make sure it's covered extremely well, as any gap will cause the brulée to scramble
5. place in a 160°C oven for 45 minutes
6. remove the moulds immediately from the water bath and allow to cool. refrigerate for at least 3-4 hours
7. slice the bananas on a diagonal and fan the slices out over the tops of the brulée

To serve, sprinkle the sugar on the top and heat with a gas torch to form a toffee crunch.

Cast

&

Crew

Absolutely fabulous
STAFF

The Three Sisters formation at Echo Point attracts visitors all year round and so do Blue Gum and Leura's Post Office Restaurants. Here's why ....

Leura

Recipes from Leura Post Office Restaurant Leura, NSW

Duck liver pâté

Makes 800g of pate

360g fresh duck livers, rinsed and connective tissue removed
250ml milk
500g heavy cream
1 whole star anise
20g salt
20g pepper
4 slices bread
80g rocket
200ml balsamic vinegar
60ml olive oil

1. Reduce the balsamic vinegar to a thick, sweet syrup
2. place livers in a bowl and pour the milk over them; allow to stand at room temperature for at least 2 hours; drain and rinse
3. pour the cream into a small saucepan; add the star anise and salt; bring to a boil, then reduce to a simmer and cook 3 minutes; remove anise
4. place the livers into a blender, then pour a small amount of the hot cream over the livers; blend to mix well
5. with the blender running, remove the cover and pour in the remaining hot cream; blend until very smooth, stopping to scrape down sides once or twice
4. add pepper and blend again; using a rubber spatula, scrape all the mixture into a medium bowl, or several small ones
5. let cool; cover tightly with plastic wrap and refrigerate at least 1 day

To finish, drizzle a zigzag across a plate. Toast the bread, cut into diamond shapes and place one piece in the centre of the prepared plate. Drizzle olive oil over it. Top with rocket. Slice a piece of pâté or make a quenelle using two large serving spoons and place this on top of the rocket. Prop up with another piece of olive soaked toast and serve.

Recipes from Blue Gum Restaurant Echo Point, NSW

Bread & butter pudding with glacé riberries

Serves 8

10 slices of bread, crusts removed
20g butter
2 bananas, sliced into rounds
5 eggs
100g caster sugar
200ml milk
500ml cream
60ml white rum
80g glacé riberries

1. Preheat the oven to 180°C
2. grease the pudding dishes with a little butter and line the bottom of the dishes with the banana slices
3. cut the bread diagonally into triangles and place these into moulds on top of the banana
4. whisk the eggs and castor sugar together, then pour in the milk, cream and rum; pour over the bread and leave to soak for about 10 to 15 minutes
5. put the dishes in a deep tray and half fill the tray with hot water; cover the whole tray with foil ensuring it does not touch the bread
6. bake for approx 25 minutes; remove the foil and cook a further 10 to 15 minutes to brown the tops
7. allow to cool

Serve topped with glacé riberries.

Alpine peppered venison
on rainforest herb linguini

This is an easy dish with very complex flavour from the herb pasta, the seasoned meat, the wild earthy mushrooms and the aromatic scented jus which you really only taste half way through the dish if it's done right. ***MM***

serves 4

1kg venison leg
1kg fresh Rainforest herb linguini (see page 182)
a large handful of English spinach
8 small pine mushrooms
10g butter
20ml Australian olive oil
Alpine Pepper
100ml game meat jus (see master recipes)
3 drops gumleaf oil

1. Trim the venison of silver and sinew (reserve for making stock)
2. cook the pasta in salted water for around eleven minutes or until al denté
3. strain the pasta, add a dash of oil and allow to cool
4. blanch the greens in water, refresh in iced water.
5. seal the venison in a hot pan and roast in a preheated oven at 200°C for 12 minutes and then rest for the same amount of time; season with Alpine Pepper
6. slice the mushrooms and sauté in a warm pan with in olive oil to which butter has been added; when the mushrooms are golden add the pasta and greens, toss until warmed through and the pasta starts to become crisp.

Place the pasta in the center of the plate. Slice the venison across the grain and lay over the pasta. Add 2-3 drops of gumleaf oil to the jus and drizzle around the plate. Venison can be garnished with a grilled and poached pear.

Lamb loin
with English spinach semi dried tomatoes and bush tomato chutney

I really enjoy cooking with lamb in general, as I find it rather versatile for every situation from roasting, BBQ'ing, pan frying or wok tossing.

During the week I take pleasure in slicing thinly then marinating some lamb fillet, then stir frying it with egg noodles, fresh crisp greens and a little Red Desert Dust. Be sure to sear the lamb quickly to ensure tenderness, add a little oyster and soy sauce to moisten the dish.

Unlike weekdays when there is little time, Sunday evenings are generally reserved for the lamb roast, which for me, consists of stuffing whole cloves of garlic, rosemary and Oz Lemon into a leg of lamb and slowly roasting it to perfection and serving with a jus lie. A jus lie is simply made adding a little red wine to the roasting pan then reducing the liquid to produce a full flavoured sauce. ***BC***

serves 4

4 x 200g lamb loin, boneless and trimmed of sinew
8 asparagus spears
12 semi dried tomatoes
200g English spinach
½ tablespoon Australian olive oil
½ tablespoon butter
100g bush tomato chutney (see master recipes)

For the sauce
500ml beef stock (see master recipes)
2ml vegetable oil
2 teaspoons Alpine Pepper

1. In a pan, add a little oil slowly sauté the Alpine Pepper for a minute; add in the stock and reduce by 80%
2. Then, with a clean steel or small knife make a hole in the centre of the lamb; stuff in the semi dried tomatoes and carefully thread through the asparagus spears
4. using butchers twine, tie up the lamb to stop it moving out of shape during cooking
5. on a hot grill or BBQ seal the lamb, fat side first; the lamb is best served medium rare, check the doneness (see our guide on page 134)
6. remove from the grill, dust with Red Desert Dust and allow to rest before cutting
7. in a small pot sauté the spinach with a little olive oil and butter

To serve, cut the lamb loins into three unequal pieces and stand these rounds upright. Garnish with tomato chutney and spinach and drizzle a little sauce around the lamb.

Wattleseed and walnut bread and butter pudding
with stewed fruits

Quandong

Quandong is an Aboriginal word of the Wiradhuri people who lived in south-west N.S.W.

Quandongs are sometimes called native peaches but the fruits have a flavour which is more like a blend of a tart apricot and peach.

Quandongs are well known to country folk for making jam or using in pies and were often dried for storage. They are available fresh, frozen and dried.

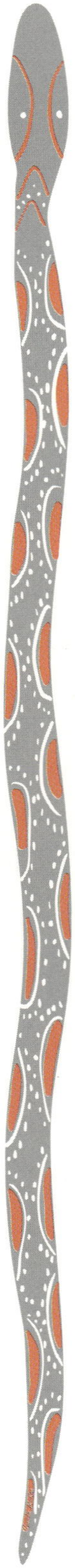

This can also utilize wattleseed and walnut bread which you might make in a bread machine adding around a tablespoonful of wattleseed to a 500g bread mix. The walnuts get added once the dough is roughly mixed and most machines have a setting for this. Bread and butter pudding is always better made on old bread and better to eat the next day or two. ***VC***

serves 4

500ml milk
500ml double cream
6 small bread rolls
40g butter
200g sugar
6 eggs
25g munthari
60g wattleseed
60g walnuts, chopped
80g quandongs
100ml honey
juice and zest from ½ orange

1. Slice the bread rolls evenly and butter each slice, with the remaining butter, line the dariole dishes
2. place the bread into the dishes together with the munthari and walnut pieces, scattered between the bread slices
3. combine the double cream, milk and wattleseed and bring to the boil in a pot
4. in a bowl cream the eggs and sugar together until firm
5. gradually add the milk and cream mixture to the eggs stirring well
6. pour the mix into the darile dishes
7. in a deep tray, lay some folded newspaper on the base and place the dariole dishes on it; fill the tray with hot water half way up the sides of the dishes and cover the whole tray with foil
8. cook in an oven at 160° for 25 minutes, remove the foil and continue cooking for another 20 minutes or until done; the custard should be set and the bread just browned
9. when cooked remove the dishes from the tray and allow to cool on the bench
10. in a small saucepan, warm the honey; add the quandong and the orange juice and zest
11. simmer for 5 minutes and allow to cool

To serve, dust with icing sugar and glazed quandongs.

Meat cookery

Here's a quick guide to check the doneness of meat as it cooks and which reflects the toughening of the protein fibres as more heat is applied over time. It will also give you a measure of the juiciness of the meat. Basically, the thumb and fingers just touch without flexing or pressing into each other. Feel the softness in the tissue at the base of the thums for a comparison as to how the meat will feel at various stages.

So, when the thumb and forefinger are touching, the soft sponginess would be equivalent to meat cooked rare. The second finger touching, firms the tissue up more to medium rare. The third finger takes it to medium and the little finger is more like well done. The juiciness follows on a decreasing scale all the way to "It's too dry to even bother eating!"

Try it out and with a little experience, you'll be able to pick the degree of doneness of a steak without even looking.

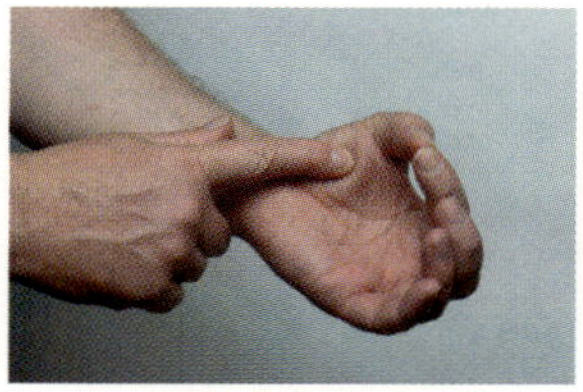

rare

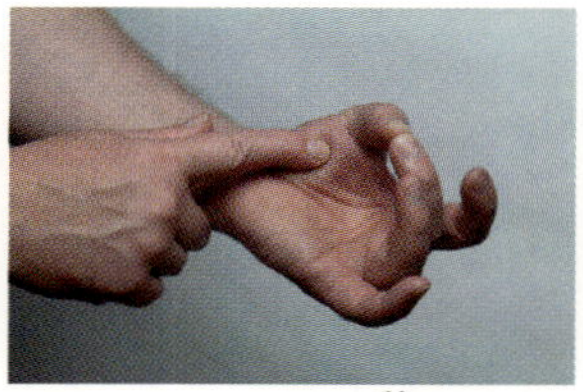

medium rare

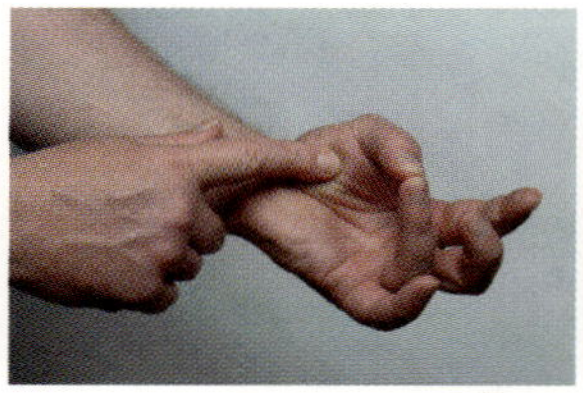

medium

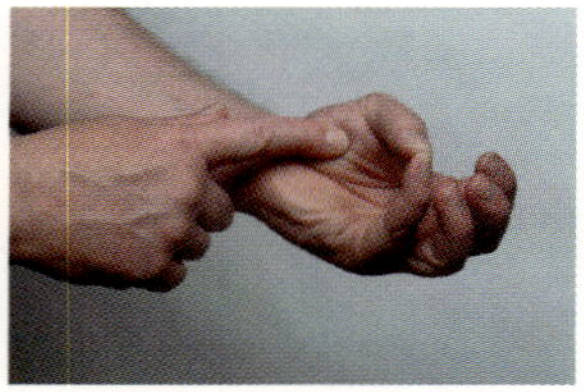

well done

The great Aussie BBQ

Nearly every house, unit or apartment in Australia has some sort of a BBQ, be it a trolley, kettle or brick version in the backyard or balcony. It's around the famous barbie where the blokes with the cold beer in the stubby holder give their missus a break from the cooking. But somehow the final product often ends up less than perfect; snags are charred, steaks are literally flame grilled and raw in the middle and all served up with burnt onions. It is generally not too impressive.

So what can we, as chefs teach you about successful cooking on the barbecue? There are endless dishes you can prepare on the BBQ so it doesn't have to be the same old steaks and snags that it's always been.

Basically, there are two ways to cook on a typical BBQ; using direct or indirect heat.

Direct cooking uses either the flat plate or char grill. It is ideal for thinner cuts of meats, poultry or seafood that are low in fat. The foods are either directly exposed to the flame, giving true BBQ flavour or exposed to the heat source on the hot plate.

Indirect cooking is more or less with a lid of some sort, where the heat circulates, cooking by convection and is ideal for large leg roasts, whole poultry or fish. This method of cooking includes roasting, smoking and rotisserie styles. As a guide, a roast at 180°C will take approx 45-50 minutes per kilo.

So let's be imaginative with what can be cooked to enhance your Saturday lunch and expand the possibilities to any day or night of the week. We'll also have a look at just what effect cooking has on the meats we throw onto the barbie in terms of food quality and enjoyment.

One of the most under-used tools for use on and around the barbie is the camp oven. You can make a damper in a camp or Bedourie oven. Flavour it with herbs, spices, fruits, cheeses, bacon - it's endless. Or use it to keep food warm or finish it cooking. But why just bake? Line the camp oven with paperbark and it turns into a mini smokehouse. Now it can turnout a constant stream of smoked oysters, scallops or fish pieces. Smoke batches of chicken, kumara or beetroot. It is even possible to smoke cheese or water which can them be used in sauces, dressings or desserts.

The paperbark can also be used as a food wrap and whole fish, chicken pieces, stuffed pork or turkey are all really good with a subtle smoke flavour. And it's no added fat cooking as well. And another thing; many people are in the habit of wrapping food as innocent as the humble potato in aluminium foil. This then gets cooked with either direct or indirect heat. Have you ever noticed when unwrapping foil potatoes just what colour the inner lining is once the potato is cooked? It tends to be dull and matt. What's happened is that the plasticisers protecting the highly reactive aluminium metal from the air have dissolved into the food and the metal has begun to corrode and oxides have been taken up into the food about to be eaten.

The problem here is twofold: Plasticisers tend to be carcinogenic being difficult for the body to eliminate as waste. Also, aluminium is potentially implicated in the Alzheimer's disease. Foil has excellent properties as a moisture barrier and has many applications in cookery but should be used without direct contact with any foodstuffs. If this proves difficult, use a barrier of baking paper or paperbark.

But back to the barbie.

So, you still want snags? Well instead of cooking regular snags, why not ask your local butcher to make some interesting sausages with native ingredients such as lamb with bush tomatoes or Australian mint, beef with riberries and Alpine Pepper or chicken or fish with Oz Lemon.

Why not dust a blue eyed cod with your favourite seasonings and then wrap it in kangaroo prosciutto and off to the grill. Or char grill king prawns and serve them with a sweet and sour lemon aspen syrup and salad.

So let's have a look at just what happens when a piece of meat goes on the barbie. How do we make or keep it tender and juicy and what can we learn about the barbecue as a cooking tool?
As soon as meat begins to heat up, the protein fibres start to tighten. This is triggered from less than 60°C and continues to maximum clench at 80°C after which, fibres begin to break leading to the loss of fluids or juices and shrinkage in the meat. It is starting to dry out on its progress from raw to not worth eating.

If we now know why meats dry out as they cook, what else is happening? Back in 1912, a French chemist by the name of Maillard described a protein sugar interaction now known as Maillard reaction. This is what's involved in caramelisation in its simplest form where pure glucose can be transformed by heat alone, into over 100 different flavour compounds including sweet and bitter compounds, sour organic acids, volatile aromatics and coloured products as well.

We also know that these reactions need high temperatures and since foods heated in liquid cannot get surface temperatures much hotter than the boiling point of water, poaching, boiling, braising and stewing all inhibit the production of Maillard flavours. And knowing that it is the browning products which impart flavour to cooked food (apart from spices, herbs, marinades etc) we start to understand more about the best way to get the most flavour out of how we cook.

For us at the barbecue, Maillard reactions have a significant impact: We generally have two places to cook easily; the grill and a hotplate. On the grill, fluids lost will drip down and keep the meat at maximum Maillard reaction rates but the juiciness is compromised. Another problem is that fat burns as the juices drip and flare up causes the temperature to drop as oxygen is consumed. The hydrocarbons in unburnt fats on the meat we are cooking appear to be detrimental to our health and the advice is to avoid open flame cooking.

At the other end of the barbie, the hotplate catches the juices running from cooking meats. This water is part of the 75% moisture content making up most meats so there's a fair bit to lose. We now know from our knowledge of Maillard chemistry that water will actually cool the temperature of the food and stop the flavour reactions happening. But on the positive side, the cooler the temperature, the less moisture lost.

So perhaps we should call the grill, the flavour maker and the hotplate, the juice saver. This might influence our cooking at the BBQ and solve the question of to sear and not to sear as well.

Research has shown that searing does not actually seal the surface of the meat. All it does is to drive the juices away from the hot surface and allow juices to later run out when the meat cools or is cut. For that matter, salting meat before cooking or not is the basis of other urban myths. Adding salt to the surface of meat might make some contribution to water movement due to the increased osmotic pull of the salty surface but moisture can only move as the proteins break down and lose their water retaining properties. The salt might pull juices to the surface but the heat drives it the other way. All in all, it probably doesn't matter when we look at the massive changes high heat causes and the relatively low temperature at which the fibres reach maximum contraction before degrading.

So we can now formulate a strategy to give us maximum flavour whilst also retaining the juiciness in meats cooked at the barbecue: Start by searing the meat on all sides on the hot grill, then move the meat to a less hot, hotplate to finish cooking more gently, while minimising water loss. When juices start to come out of the meat, move it to a drier area on the hotplate. Keeping the heat up with a little oil is fine but moving away from juices on the hotplate is more important.

It is still important to rest meat which has been direct heated so that juices can redistribute somewhat before the muscle is cut. This will reduce the loss of juices from the side furthest from the hotplate. The camp oven which we hope will find its way to becoming an essential element of your outdoor cooking, is ideal for this resting stage.

Lastly, avoid dousing the meat on the hotplate with marinade leftovers or salting with soy or other sauces. While it will deglaze the hotplate, there are limited Maillard products on it. Your fried onions are proof of this as they rarely brown to crispness but sweat, go translucent and generally pick up carbon deposits more than caramelisation products. You are better off adding sauces to the rested meats or to the plate on serving.

Australian Fruit Spice ~ a seasoning developed for Dining Downunder by Vic Cherikoff

Add a wild burst of fruit

Spicemaster notes:

COLOUR - visually mixed green herb fines and pieces including micro-crystals of natural flavour and with flecks of dark purple fruity spices

AROMA - passionfruit and berry front notes with a hint of cumin and the tiniest suggestion of caroway

PALATE - full-on fruit to match the aroma and with a subtle pepper and anise long palate

STORAGE - chilled storage recommended

This is a really unique seasoning for enhancing the natural fruit flavour of soft or stone fruits such as berries, apricots, peaches or tropical fruits like mango. I also use it to make ordinary fruit jams and jellies more fruity. It only takes a light sprinkle, stir it in and wait for a few minutes for the flavour to infuse. It takes less time if the product is warm to hot.

If you purée fruit for dessert sauces or make syrups from cooked fruit and sugar, Fruit Spice will add a delicious strawberry-passionfruit character with a subtle lemony hint.

And here's a really good recipe for a salad dressing - one which I still use often. Blend some strawberries and add Fruit Spice by the pinch, to taste. You might even add a bit of cracked black pepper. Now, if you are serving a salad of interesting green leaves such as radicchio, cos, rocket, coral, baby beetroot leaves, cresses and more, you can dress it well ahead of time with this Fruit spice and juice mix. You see, if you use an oil based dressing, the oil wilts the leaves quickly unlike juices which actually make the leaves more turgid or pumped up. I once cooked a lunch for 60 chefs as a demonstration meal and made this dressing so that I could prepare the salad hours beforehand and just chill the salad covered in plastic wrap. It looked better than when I made it and tasted so good I had nearly all 60 chefs ask what I used to flavour the leaves. What better recommendation?

I love using this mix in yoghurt, custards and whipped cream and think that it makes one of the best ice creams you will ever try.

Fruit spice by the generous pinch also turns up the gain on vegetable casseroles and other wet dishes using pumpkin, sweet potato or kumara. If you thoughtfully smell Fruit Spice and hunt around in your brain's smell library you might be able to detect some of the aromas behind the primary passionfruit and strawberry notes. To me, they suggest caraway and cumin and it is these which make a fruity Asian or Indian curry come to life!

The pairing of fruit and meat is common to many traditional Aboriginal cuisines. It was a feature in the cooking styles of many quite different, regional groups; from rainforest people in the tropical north to desert dwellers in the arid centre of the continent, people who had never seen forests or the ocean (for that matter never see rain - some outback people would have lived a healthy 45-60 years, right through an 80 year drought). In any event, any meat sauce or fruit and meat combination will be deliciously enhanced with a light seasoning of Fruit Spice.

This venue is a feast for the senses; from the stunning beach views to the food prepared by Chef and owner, André Chouvin and his team of 7 chefs.

Avoca beach

Recipes from Feast Avoca Beach, NSW

Lamb loin and ratatouille

Serves 1

2 roma tomatoes
1 zucchini
rice stick noodles, deep fried as a garnish
1 eggplant, finely diced
1 tomato, finely diced
1 zucchini, finely diced
1 onion, finely diced
1 clove garlic, squashed and minced
seasonings, salt, pepper, Alpine Pepper
180g lamb loin, fully trimmed
60ml lamb jus
10ml cream

You will need a ring mould of around 12cm diameter

1. For the top garnish, pour boiling water over the roma tomatoes and after a few minutes remove their skins
2. slice the tomatoes down their length and remove the seeds
3. slice the zucchini on the diagonal to match the size of the roma tomato pieces
4. arrange these two vegetables in an alternate pattern to make an over-lapping wheel about 12cm diameter; brush with Australian olive oil and place in a warm oven for 12 hours to semi-dry them
5. reduce the lamb stock to a jus or keep the jus warm, stirring occasionally, add cream and Alpine Pepper before serving
6. make the ratatouille by stir-frying the onion and garlic in vegetable oil until the onion is translucent; salt the onion
7. add the eggplant, tomato and zucchini and cook down to soften all the vegetables; add a pinch of Alpine Pepper
8. sear the lamb loin all over and finish to medium rare in the oven at 160°C for 10 minutes. Remove and leave to rest for 10 minutes before slicing on a diagonal across the grain
9. set the mould in the middle of the plate and fill with ratatouille to about 2.5cm
10. arrange a spiral of the lamb slices on top of the lamb and set the semi-dried tomato arrangement on top

Serve garnished with a deep-fried noodle nest and the jus ringed around the food.

"a feast for the senses...."

Barralax
on rainforest herb linguini

Outback salt

This is produced from the sun-dried underground brines in the Murray Darling Basin.

The salt produced contains the naturally occurring minerals as well as other elements from the brine resulting in a different taste to ordinary sodium chloride.

The underground saline waters have been rising towards the surface as a result of land clearing. So in utilizing these waters, the environment is improved and a unique salt is available as a gourmet product.

Should it be barralax or gravamundi? Either is a corruption of the Scandinavian word for the process of dry curing salmon – but we wanted to make it our own using what is often considered amongst the best eating fish around. This dish needs to be prepared well ahead of time as the curing of the barramundi can take up to 24 hours. ***MM***

serves 4

4 baby barramundi fillets, skinless
1 cup sugar
1 cup salt (common table salt is fine here)
2 teaspoons Alpine Pepper
250g rainforest herb linguini (see pasta recipe 182)
Australian olive oil
½ tablespoon butter
2 red capsicums roasted and peeled
100g snow peas
100g English spinach or warrigal greens
2 teaspoons Oz Lemon

1. Combine the salt and sugar
2. in a deep tray, spread about a third of the mix, place the fillets on top and pack with the remaining cure mix
3. leave for 2 hours at room temperature or chill for 24 hours
4. when the barramundi flesh has firmed up and lightened in colour, rinse it in fresh water, drain and dry throughly on paper toweling
5. slice into thin pieces cutting across the fillets at an angle of 30°
6. prepare the pasta in salted boiling water for 11 minutes or until al denté, drain and add a dash of olive oil (Australian, of course)
7. top and tail the snow peas removing the string from the edges
8. blanch the snow peas and warrigal greens and refresh in iced water then drain
9. slice the capsicums into thin strips
10. heat up a wok add a little oil and a nob of butter, toss the pasta until golden then add the snow peas, greens and capsicums, dish up the 4 serves
11. to the hot pan, add the barralax slices, toss for about 1 minute; sprinkle with Oz Lemon and serve on top of the rainforest herb linguini

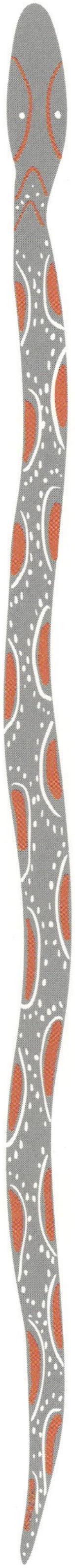

Wine drenched lamb
with Alpine Pepper mash

I love tender lamb with a good drop of red, so here I would recommend using a light red wine, as marinating it in a strong full bodied merlot or cabernet sauvignon will make it difficult to pair with a table wine to go with the meal. The strong peppery notes of the Alpine Pepper creates a unique flavour with plenty of punch. ***BC***

serves 4

180g lamb loin
1 cup red wine
80g potatoes
80ml lamb stock
50g green beans
50g asparagus
10g Rainforest Rub
2g Outback Salt
5g Alpine Pepper
20g butter
50ml cream
5ml vegetable oil

1. Marinate the lamb in a small bowl with the wine for about 5-6 hours or overnight in the fridge
2. peel and roughly chop the potatoes and place in a pot; cover generously with cold water and bring to the boil; simmer for 35 minutes or until soft
3. remove the lamb from the red wine and on a hot BBQ or grill, seal and brown the meat allover; finish in the oven at 180°C for 12 minutes; rest the meat for 10 minutes
4. combine the remaining red wine marinade with the lamb jus and reduce to a thick sauce; be sure to strain the jus before serving
5. strain the potatoes and mash together with butter and cream, season with salt and Alpine Pepper
6. slice the asparagus and green beans
7. heat a large frying pan or wok with a little vegetable oil, sauté the green beans and asparagus and finish with Rainforest Rub

Slice the lamb and serve on the potato mash with the greens to the side and the plate drizzled with the lamb jus.

Wattleseed pavlova

This has to be a contender for an Australian national dish. Even if the Kiwis simultaneously concocted the same sort of meringue mixture, the idea of serving it in Swiss roll fashion instead of as a cow pat must put us in front. ***VC***

serves 4

7 egg whites
1 teaspoon lemon juice
1 tablespoon corn flour
1¼ cups castor sugar
300ml whipped cream
2 tablespoons Wattleseed extract
½ cup crumbed Dick Smith Foods' Bushfood Breakfast cereal or biscuit crumbs
strawberry jam
juice of 1 lemon
¼ teaspoon Fruit Spice

1. Add the Wattleseed extract to the cream and whip this to stiff peaks; this can and is best done the day before to allow the full flavour to develop; taste and add more extract if you want a stronger flavour
2. whip the egg whites to soft peaks; add the sugar and lemon juice slowly until stiff peaks form
3. line a baking tray with baking paper to cover an area the width of the baking paper and 1¼ times the length
4. spread the pavlova mix over the baking paper in a rectangular shape to a depth of 2cm
5. bake at 150°C for 10 to 15 minutes or until firm and nearly touch dry but not browned; it should look like soft meringue at this stage
6. remove from the oven and slide it off the tray to stop it cooking on; sprinkle the top with the crumbed breakfast cereal evenly coating the surface.
7. flip the meringue over, seasoned side down, onto a clean tea towel and remove the baking paper carefully; if it sticks, place a wet towel which has been heated in a microwave (or soaked with really hot water) on to the baking paper for 30 seconds; try peeling the paper away again and it should come away cleanly
8. spread the Wattle cream evenly over the meringue to a thickness of around 1cm or ½ an inch
9. roll up the pavlova using the long edge of the towel; cut the ends on an angle (good cooks will selflessly taste-test the trimmings)
10. before removing the towel completely, lift the pavlova onto a platter and roll the pavlova off the towel

Serve with a sour fruit coulis, for example, a berry jam mixed with enough lemon juice to taste tart and to pour like a thick sauce. I'd add a pinch of Fruit Spice to this sauce as well to enhance the fruitiness.

High up on the ridge, overlooking the surf beach of Terrigal, we found The Cowrie which specializes in seafood.

Terrigal beach

Recipes from Cowrie Restaurant Terrigal, NSW

Seafood Platter

Serves 4

12 king prawns
8 Balmain bugs
8 oysters
8 slices of smoked salmon
2 whole sand crabs
4 scampi or yabbies
2 lobsters
2 kiwi fruit
8 strawberries
200g rock melon
2 passionfruit
1 dragonfruit

The seafood plate is so easy to prepare and can be easily changed depending on what is available.

1. Prepare the cooked seafood, cutting the bugs and lobsters in half and cleaning the sand crabs
2. cut the rockmelon, passionfruit, kiwi and dragon fruit
3. place the seafood with the fruits and garnish with strawberries

Serve with Wildfire mayonnaise (see master recipes)

Tagine of mixed seafood

Serves 2

6 mussels in the shell
2 x 80g snapper fillets
1 Balmain bug, halved
4 prawns
2 scampi
20g bush tomato chutney (see masters recipes)
50ml fish stock
20ml white wine
50g cous cous
12 chickpeas, soaked
1 clove garlic, crushed and minced
10ml olive oil
5g butter
2g salt
2g pepper
10g parmesan cheese

1. To a hot pan, add a little olive oil, butter and garlic; then add all the seafood and sauté for 2 minutes
2. add the bush tomato chutney, white wine, fish stock, chickpeas and couscous
3. bring to a simmer, then place in the oven for 10 minutes at 170°C
4. season with salt and pepper

Serve in a tagine dish and finish with parmesan cheese.

Steamed blue eyed cod with fennel and king prawns

Serves 1

200g blue eyed cod (skin on)
50g fennel
2 king prawns
50ml white wine
40g leek
10g flour
2g salt

1. In a small pan place the fennel and then put both king prawns on top of the fennel; add the white wine and place on the heat
2. ensure the blue eyed cod is free from bones; using another pan seal the cod fillet, skin side first for about 2 minutes, then remove and place on top of the king prawns
3. cover the pan with foil and place in the oven for 12 minutes at 170°C
4. while the cod is cooking, prepare the leek, by finely slicing it
5. dust with flour and deep fry in hot oil until crispy; be careful when you add the leeks as the oil can bubble up quickly, so add small amounts at a time

Remove the cod and transfer both the broth and cod into a bowl. Serve with crispy leeks on top.

Shellfish paella
with lemon aspen fruits

I guess every chef in the world has their own paella recipe. Traditionally, paella has chorizo sausages, saffron, olives, chicken, mussels and parsley. In some ways it's like a risotto that is open ended, where you can add anything that tickles your fancy.

In the studio I cooked up different native paella for the crew with emu proscuitto, squid, chicken, kangaroo sausage all flavoured with bush tomato chutney and Alpine Pepper using the same base recipe. ***BC***

serves 4

8 x 50g snapper fillets
8 medium scallops
8 king prawns
2 squid tubes
100g bush tomato chutney (see master recipes)
80g parmesan cheese
2 shallots
60g butter
8 lemon aspen fruits
300g of arborio or medium grain rice
20g Red Desert Dust
1 litre fish stock
50ml white wine
15ml olive oil
5g Outback Salt

1. In a paella or wide saucepan heat a little butter and olive oil, shallots and Red Desert Dust on low heat; then add rice to the pan and sauté until translucent
2. when the rice grains are translucent add in the white wine, bush tomato chutney then the stock; place on low heat and allow the rice to cook slowly.
3. while the rice is gently cooking away, begin to prepare the seafood; remove any bones from the snapper fillets, peel and de-vein the de-headed prawns and slice in half
4. cut the squid tubes into bite sized pieces and score these with diagonal, parallel cross cuts; unless the scallops are still in the shell, they require little if any preparation
5. heat up a hot plate or BBQ for all the seafood; place on the snapper and prawns first, and then put on the scallops and squid as these take very little time to cook; by cooking the seafood this way, it gives the paella a smoky flavour which is usually imparted by the addition of Spanish chorizo sausage in more traditional paella
6. try and cook all the seafood about three quarters the way through, this will ensure that when they are placed in the paella they are not overcooked and tough; add the seafood to the rice, as well as lemon aspen fruits; check the doneness of the rice and the consistency of the paella; a guide is to have risotto like consistency, yet enough liquid to form a sauce
7. when the seafood has been added, add half of the parmesan cheese, ensure you reserve some to top on each serve; taste and add salt where required

Serve in a deep or soup bowl, with a generous serve of parmesan cheese on top.

Arborio rice

Rissotto rice, short grain or Arborio rice is used to make the dish risotto. This old world method involves stirring hot liquid little by little into the rice for about 20 minutes.

Risotto is prepared this way and served immediately to preserve the unique, gourmet texture of a very creamy sauce around al dente, pasta-like rice kernels.

Once you have the risotto base, it can be flavoured with various ingredients such as scallop, Oz Lemon and parmesan cheese.

Twice baked goats cheese soufflé

Experiment with this dish; add what ever you want to the soufflé, sweet or savory it doesn't matter. And try the more ripen cheeses which can handle other strong flavours Unlike a conventional souffle which is light and fluffy, this twice cooked version is a little more substantial and well as being delicious. ***MM***

serves 4

40g butter
225ml milk
1 bay leaf
1 pinch grated nutmeg
½ onion, sliced
40g flour
175g ripe goat's cheese
4x 60g eggs separated
½ teaspoon Alpine Pepper
150ml cream

1. Preheat the oven to 180°C
2. using a thick bottomed pan melt the butter slowly
3. in a separate pan warm the milk, bay leaf, nutmeg and onion gently
4. add the flour to the butter and cook out for about 1 minute, stirring
5. add the soft goats cheese and stir until it combines
6. add the egg yolks
7. whip the egg whites in an electric mixer, a good tip when working with egg whites is to wipe the bowl out with a lemon half, and start the egg whites off slowly; this helps them to take in more air, then turn the speed to full until the whites are firm and you could upturn the bowl above your head without wearing egg on your face
8. add the milk to the cheese mixture and cook out, stirring until all the lumps have gone; season with the Alpine Pepper and then take the pan off the heat so that it cools down
9. butter and flour six moulds
10. fold in one spoonful of the whipped egg whites at a time, so that you don't lose the aeration, be gentle and the result will be great
11. spoon the mixture into the moulds and place in a deep tray; add boiling water ¾ way up the sides of the moulds
12. put them in the pre heated oven for about twenty minutes; remove and allow to cool

When it is time to serve the soufflés, pour the cream over them and place them back in the oven until warm. I like to serve these soufflés with a really peppery, rocket (choose the older leaves rather than baby rocket which is too mild for this dish) and dress it with a balsamic reduction and some diced fresh chilli.

Ashed goats cheese

Ashed Goats cheese is a mild goats cheese which is covered in a fine edible ash, typically from made from wine vines.

The ash itself is tasteless and extends the life of the cheese, however some people tend to cut or peel away the ash.

Australia is starting to produce exceptional goats cheeses, most of which are coming out of Western Australia, Victoria and Tasmanian regions.

Australian Alpine Pepper ~ a seasoning developed for Dining Downunder by Vic Cherikoff

An aromatic pepper mix with a slow burn to ignite your tastebuds

Spicemaster notes:

COLOUR - olive and pastel green herb pieces with flecks of dark purple millings of fruits of the spices; sumac and pepperberries

AROMA - woody peppery note with a hint of fruit

PALATE - herbaceous short palate with conventional pepper zing then exhibiting an increasing burn with rich berry and a hint of green tea

STORAGE - chilled storage recommended

You may think that you have tried all the varieties of pepper before but here is a totally new one. Sure. There's black, grey and white pepper as well as green, pink and red pepper which all come from the same plant (a climber, originally from India). You may have even tried betel pepper, Indian or Javan long peppers or the rough-leaved pepper - all are different species of the same genus; Piper.

However, here in Australia, we have a totally new type of pepper which is more closely related to the original plant source of aspirin or Oil of Wintergreen than to the tropical true pepper vine. We call it mountain pepper and it's actually a herb although the berries or pepperberries as they are known, are also used as a spice - sparingly. I say this because chewing on a few berries is like having a grenade go off in your mouth.

My Alpine Pepper is a carefully considered formulation of the peppery leaves of mountain pepper along with some of the dried and milled fruits of this high country shrub. Think of the fiery leaves, draped in snow in the winter and blasted by Antarctic winds which kiss the icy valleys where this tough plant grows. I also include a specially prepared, encapsulated extract of the leaves which imparts that instant zing of bushy heat. There's some aniseed myrtle which not only ideally complements the taste but adds to some serious functionality in that the combination is super-strongly anti-microbial so that there is some preservative action when using Alpine Pepper as a marinade. Finally, I have added an amalgamation of the tangy, Middle Eastern sumac for its fruitiness to enhance the same flavour from the pepperberries and the conventional Piper corns in their black and white forms are added for those familiar pepper notes.

It won't be long before you'll reach for Alpine Pepper as most cooks would for a peppermill. It can easily and deliciously substitute for ordinary pepper on meats, seafood, soups, vegetables, eggs and cheese dishes. Use it to taste and you'll discover that Wow! Factor you want in your food.

But Alpine Pepper can also be used in far more ways than just as a seasoning over cooked dishes. Use it as a dry marinade on meats or add it to breads, batter and pastry as a herb mix. It makes the best salt and pepper squid I have ever tried.

Now here's something discovered by accident - Try sprinkling Alpine Pepper over raw or cooked fruit or mix it into ice cream (particularly strawberry flavoured), yoghurt, cream cheese or custards. Alternatively, generously season peeled and sliced bananas with Alpine Pepper and pan-fry them in butter and a dash of your favorite oil (olive, macadamia, avocado, walnut, pumpkin seed, whatever) until they just brown and soften. Serve with ice cream and a small cup of strong coffee.

By the way, I store my Alpine Pepper on the door of my refrigerator (in fact all my seasonings are there). It keeps the aromatics fresh and means they are always at hand and won't go the way of less valued spices which get buried and lost or just ignored and forgotten in my pantry cupboards.

Finally, if you can't get Alpine Pepper, you could use ordinary black pepper as a substitute and mix in some milled anise, a generous proportion of white pepper, a little sumac and a dash of Szechwan pepper. Unfortunately, it won't be the same.

Munthari

Munthari are small, fragrant, apple-flavoured berries from a beach creeper common on dunes in southern South Australia. Also called muntries, emu apples or native cranberries, munthari can be used in salads, sauces and pies or eaten just as they come. Their production is still in its infancy with total harvests rarely exceeding a few tonne.

Aniseed myrtle

Aniseed myrtle leaves are harvested from a rare plant originally found in north coast New South Wales and south-east Queensland rainforests. The commercially available variety is only harvested from artificially propagated plants and is still very limited in availability. Use native aniseed in a similar fashion to lemon myrtle leaves.

Sugarbag

Sugarbag is a widely used colloquial Aboriginal-English name for the honey from native bees. The name came from the comparison to the white bushman's sugar which always came in a bag. Native bees are found all over Australia except in parts of the arid centre. Here Aborigines harvested honey ants, gum exudates and lerp as their sweet foods. Recently, artificial hives have been designed to successfully house native bees. These hives can be designed as breeding boxes which are easily split when full. Alternatively, a honey chamber can be added to the top of the hive and honey harvested each year. Bees in the warmer climates may make up to a litre of honey each year, whereas in Sydney the bees only go out to gather nectar once the temperature goes over 16 to 18°C. Southern bees thus have shorter working hours and probably harvest nectar at a slower pace than bees in the tropics and sub-tropics.

This production from native hives may be very small by comparison to the feral European bee but the quality of the honey is high. The taste of sugarbag can be described as bitter-sweet with the mellowness of a smooth port wine and a pleasant, resinous character.

The Rocks
ARGE LIFESTYLE
MBO
1844
HOTEL

Hidden up in the tangled lanes and walkways of Sydney's colonial past, we found Aboriginal owned and run, Lillipilli in the Rocks

The Rocks

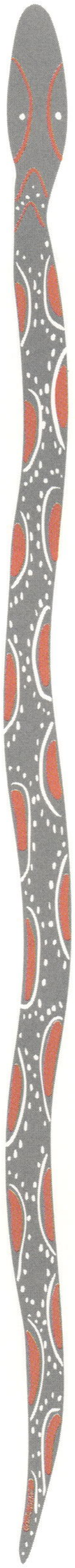

Wattled croc
with lime and riberry jam

There is a satisfaction in eating something that wouldn't think twice about eating you, given half the chance! And harvesting crocodiles for meat is part of good resource management.

One of the few flavours which enhances rather than overwhelms the very subtle, fishy-chicken flavour of crocodile is wattle. This is one occasion that wattle is used dry as a seasoning rather than more commonly being boiled first to soften the grounds and extract its characteristic flavour. ***VC***

serves 4

For the croc

1 kg crocodile tail fillet (bone out and trimmed)
60g wattle
Outback Salt
1 piece damp paperbark, appropriately thinned
string or cooking twine

For the meat jam

100g large wild limes
100g riberries
200ml water
¼ teaspoon Outback Salt
75g sugar

For the croc

1. In a bowl, sprinkle the crocodile with the wattle to evenly coat the meat and lightly season with salt
2. roll the meat to form a log shape and set in the middle of the paperbark sheet; wrap well and tie securely
3. place in a microwave dish and cook on high (750W) for 5 minutes; rest for 5 minutes, invert the roll and cook a further 5 minutes on high; alternatively, poach in a steam oven until firm to touch, although this will give a drier result as the juices tend to run with prolonged cooking
4. chill overnight then remove the bark from the required amount of crocodile (re-wrap and chill the remainder)
5. machine slice the crocodile to 2mm thickness

For the meat jam

1. Finely slice the limes
2. boil and then simmer both fruits in the water until the lime skins soften (about 40 minutes) if more water is required then add a little at a time
3. with the salt to balance the bitterness of the limes and sugar to sweeten to taste; this is designed to be a very tart, powerful lime flavoured jam ideal for savoury applications

Fan out 35 to 40g portions around the relish. Serve with the meat jam and green garnish.

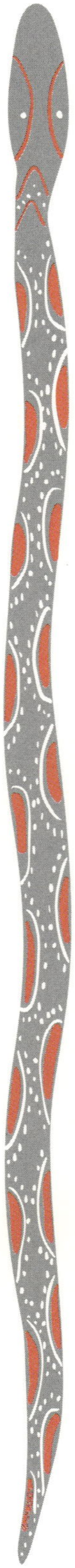

Pork braise

with bunya nut and Australian rice grass

This recipe is a little ahead of its time in that it has an ingredient, Australian rice grass, which is only just entering commercialization stages.

It may be a few more years before it is widely available but small amounts are beginning to enter selected gourmet stores. A substitute is the Canadian wild rice harvested and widely marketed as Inuit rice but it is really closer to the nutty dryland rice grasses of Arizona in the USA. ***MM***

serves 4

4 pork hocks
3 litres chicken stock
1 onion diced
1 chopped chilli
½ teaspoon Wildfire Spice
½ teaspoon Oz Lemon
1½ teaspoons Alpine Pepper
200g brown rice
50g Australian rice grass
50g Inuit wild rice
12 bunya nuts (24 halves)
160g snowpeas

1. Preheat your oven or BBQ to about 180°C
2. stab the meat of the hocks with a narrow blade knife making an incision which fits your finger; sprinkle Alpine Pepper into the cuts so that the flavours can penetrate all the way through the meat as it cooks
3. in a hot, oiled, deep roasting pan, brown the hocks on all surfaces to flavour the outside; once half done, add the onion to brown it as well
4. once browned, remove from the heat and pour in the stock and add the chilli
5. cover the meat with aluminium foil ensuring that the plasticized metal sheet does not touch the meat but sits proud; if this is not possible, cover the meat with a piece of baking paper or paperbark and then cover with the foil; (the main thing is to never let anything you will actually eat, be cooked in contact with foil, see page 134)
6. place in the oven for 2-3 hours or until the meat easily pulls away from the bone; the pan can be uncovered for the last 30 minutes of this time (when you can also start to cook the rice as below)
7. once the hocks are cooked, remove them from the liquid and set aside in a warm place
8. pull all of the meat away from the bones
9. reduce the liquid in the pan to ¼ the original volume; strain off and season this sauce with Wildfire Spice to taste
10. boil the bunya nut halves in a minimum of water and then allow them to cool in this water, this will make it easy to get them out of the shells; use almonds if bunya nuts are hard to get and you can boil them or dry roast them as is your preference, either way, chop the nuts coarsely
11. start to cook the rices:
12. add the brown rice and the rice grass to a saucepan which can be fitted with a lid; cover the rice with water so that the water covers the rice by 1½ times as much again as the depth of rice; said in another way; you can measure the 200g of rice and add 300ml of water; note that if you were cooking white rice using this absorption method only 200ml of water would be needed
13. for the rice grass (or Inuit wild rice), follow the above directions as for white rice and use a small saucepan
14. to cook the rices, bring the water to the boil and continue boiling until the water boils down to within the surface of the rice; turn the heat down to a gentle simmer and fit the lid to the saucepan; continue simmering for 10 minutes or until the rice is cooked as indicated by 'blow hole' in the surface of the swollen rice; remove from heat once done; place the snow peas ontop of the rice and cover till required to serve.

Serve the rices in a deep or flat bowl, topped with the braised pork, bunya and snow peas. Dust with Alpine Pepper.

Rainforest lime
and macadamia nut pudding

Slightly spicy, sweet and sour is how I describe this Rainforest lime dessert pudding with macadamia nuts. The spicy sweet flavours come from the ginger marmalade and the sourness is from the wild limes.

If you can't get hold of Australian native limes, you can substitute them with regular limes. Make sure to remove the rind and the seeds or it'll be too bitter to eat. This is not necessary if you are using the fully edible rainforest limes. ***BC***

serves 4

50g chopped macadamia nuts
135g butter
75g soft brown sugar
2 tablespoons Buderim ginger, lemon and lime marmalade
½ teaspoon Oz Lemon
150g rainforest limes, sliced whole
120g self-raising flour
½ teaspoon Outback salt
120g castor sugar
2 eggs, beaten

1. Dry roast the chopped nuts until the fines just begin to darken
2. melt 15g butter in a pan, add the brown sugar and marmalade, stir well to dissolve the sugar; remove from heat and sprinkle in the Oz Lemon
3. butter a deep ovenproof dish and pour in the mixture; place the slices of limes over this mixture
4. in a bowl, sieve the flour and salt
5. in another bowl, beat the castor sugar with the remaining butter, add the eggs and flour gradually, stirring well
6. pour this mix carefully over the fruit and bake at 180°C for 35 minutes

When cooked, turn out on a dish so that the limes are on top or serve from the bowl. The mix will be pudding soft in the centre and really good to eat with ice cream or cream.

Paper bark

Paperbark is a useful natural biodegradable material which can replace greaseproof paper, baking paper, oven bags, plastic wrap and aluminium foil. Paperbark imparts a delicate smoke flavour which is particularly noticeable with poultry, pork or freshwater fish. Vegetables can also be wrapped and baked in paperbark and the whole package served at the table. Serveral of our recipes also show how to line platters with paperbark for finger food served Aboriginal style.

Bunya nut

Similar to a European chestnut (even nutritionally) with a subtle pine overtone, these large, low fat, starchy nuts are protected by a woody shell and come from an ancient pine which once grew right along the eastern seaboard. However, by the time of whites invaded Australia, the bunya bunya pine had reduced its range to two disparate communities in Queensland; the Bunya Mountains near Kingaroy, and a small region near Rockhampton. They were widely planted in the late 1880's and again spread along the east coast and even to South Australia.

To remove the meat from halved nuts simply bring the nuts to a boil in a minimum quantity of water. Leave to cool and as the nut meat swells it often eases out of the shell in the process. If not, it is an easy matter to pry out the meat, reserving the woody shells to smoke meats, fish, poultry and vegetables or use as a mould for re-fried nut purée.

This last product is undoubtedly the best way of preparing bunya nuts in that it makes the most of the very complex, high temperature, protein-starch reactions called Maillard products. These are familiar to us as the flavour of caramelised sugar, toasted bread and bread crust, roast meats and nuts, dark beer, chocolate, coffee, wattle and more.

To prepare re-fried bunya nut purée, blend the de-shelled nuts in the water in which they were boiled. Add enough water to make a thick purée. Add a source of fat such as thickened cream, butter or oil and extend if you wish with wheat, barley or some other flour. Transfer to an oiled saucepan and cook on high heat while constantly stirring and scraping the browning purée. Keep cooking (making Maillard products) until the purée forms a roux and begins to leave the sides of the pan. It will have a pale, pinky straw colour and a far more pronounced flavour than the raw nut meat.

Use this roux as a pie or tart crust, as dumplings, garnishes or if sweetened during the process, the paste can be worked back into the half shells which you line with plastic wrap, popped out as a mock nut and chocolate coat them decoratively as a dessert garnish.

Science gives us some clues as to the recipe here since Maillard products are produced at high temperatures and water can only reach 100°C. the browning accelerates once the water is cooked out of the purée. (Hence only use a small amount of the cooking water to blend up the nuts or use oil – cream will often curdle from the rough treatment so this is best added to the nuts once puréed).

Wattleseed

The Australian Egg Board (a now defunct, semi government authority which was charged with marketing eggs and egg products) and particularly, one Hilary Wright,at the time was instrumental in developing this dessert concept as a way to use egg whites but the Wattleseed cream only came about after my accidental discovery of how to roast these amazing seeds.

In brief, it was 1984 and I was trying to heat parch a range of Acacia seeds to mimic the process Aborigines employ to make the seeds grind to a powder instead of a pasty meal (compare grinding dry wheat to a flour as against trying to mill (squash?) unripe, green wheat grains). Anyway. While I was roasting the seeds of a particular species of Acacia on the stove top, the phone rang. Simply taking the pan off the heat while I headed off to answer the phone call did not stop the seeds from continuing to roast on and when I came back it looked as though I had thoroughly burnt the small black seeds. However, before ditching them and starting again and by a stroke of fate, I let the seeds cool. I also wanted to test if they would be easier to grind to a powder in this condition than the raw seeds which, incidentally, were as hard as small stones. Well. When I took the lid of my small, Italian coffee grinder after 'whizzing the Wattle a while', up came this delicious aroma of coffee, chocolate and hazelnut all toasty and rich.

A few moments later the world's first Acaccino™ was born as I spooned the milk froth over my just brewed, wattleseed extract. It didn't take long for this exquisite flavour to find its way into ice cream, custard, bread, whipped cream and chocolates. Oh. And it adds a rich, cleansing nuttiness to quality ale as well. See beverage suggestions on page 173

Our famous beach is home to a wide choice of places to eat and drink, from the Swiss Grand to Moorish bar and all with a beach front view.

Bondi

Recipes from The Swiss Grand Bondi Beach, NSW

Baby barramundi wrapped in paperbark

Serves 1

30cm x 40cm piece of paperbark
15cm x 15cm piece of banana leaf
2 x 80g baby barramundi fillets
2g lemon myrtle
10g vegetable oil
160g kumara
10g butter
20ml cream
50g English spinach

1. For the kumara mash, roughly chop the kumara and place in a pot together with cold salted water and bring to the boil
2. to make the paperbark wrap; line the paperbark with banana leaf, this is more for decoration but does lessen the barramundi sticking to the bark
3. place one of the fillets skin side down; sprinkle a little Oz Lemon; place the other fillet head to tail on top, this time skin side up
4. fold the banana leaf over the fish and then the paperbark and wrap to form a small parcel; place on a pan and bake in a hot oven at 180°C for 12-15 minutes
5. while the barramundi is cooking, finish off the kumara mash by straining and mashing the cooked kumara together with the butter and cream
6. in a hot pan, add a little oil and wilt the English spinach

To serve, plate up the spinach next to the barramundi parcel and 3 quenelles of kumara mash. Serve with Illawarra plum salsa or bush tomato chutney. Tear open the paperbark parcel at the table.

Kangaroo fillet with mango chutney, cherries and sweet potato mash

Serves 1

1 x 180g kangaroo, wallaby or emu fillet
30g mango chutney
50g white sweet potato
½ small Spanish onions
oil for frying
2g fresh dill
salt and pepper
60ml beef jus
20g de-seeded dark cherries
5ml cream

1. Dice the sweet potatoes
2. in a lightly oiled pan add the Spanish onions, sauté till golden; add sweet potato dice and toss until golden; add fresh dill and mango chutney; continue to sauté till thick, then remove from the heat
3. prepare the kangaroo fillet by rubbing salt and pepper into the meat
4. in another hot oiled pan, sear the fillet all over to brown; finish in a hot oven for 6 to 8 minutes to no more than medium rare; remove from heat and allow to rest for 10 minutes
5. in another small pan, prepare the sauce by combining the beef jus and cherries; reduce slightly

On the plate and using a mould, place the sweet potato and mango mix into the mould. Once the kangaroo has rested, slice it across the grain on an angle. Place the slices over the sweet potato and mango mix. Around the edges spoon on the cherry sauce and garnish with drops of cream.

From Moorish Restaurant and Bar

There are many weird and wonderful drinks possible with the vast array of alcoholic beverages on the market but several are always popular irrespective of the trends of the day. Maybe it's because of James Bond but the martini is eternal. There is no passing up a beer on a hot day, overlooking the view at Bondi Beach and these flavoured beers are really interesting. Try them yourself soon. And lastly, the Bloody Mary is reborn to the Moorish Mary named after the restaurant in which Mark Ward resides as expert barman/creator of these concoctions.

Riberry Martini

45ml vodka
10ml riberry syrup
3 barspoons of glacé riberries
dash of cranberry juice
hint of lime
ice

Combine all ingredients, shake.

Lighthouse Lemon Ale
3 drops of soluble lemon myrtle oil
a schooner of light beer

Wattleseed Light
10ml wattleseed extract
a schooner of light beer

Simply put the flavour into the poured pilsner and serve.

Moorish Mary

1 part vodka
3 parts tomato juice
4 barspoons Bush tomato chutney
a few dashes of Worcestershire sauce
a pinch of celery salt
a dash of celery juice (optional)
a dash of lemon juice
a generous sprinkle of Wildfire Spice
Red Desert Dust
lemon and cucumber slices for garnish

Blend together the vodka tomato juice and bush tomato chutney. Add the sauce, salt, juices and pour into a glass rimmed with Red Desert Dust and carefully filled with ice. Stir gently. Top the Moorish Mary with the Wildfire Spice and garnish with slices of cucumber and lemon.

Wild Lime Caipiroska

60ml vodka
6 wild limes
2 barspoons of white sugar
Ice

Crush the wild limes together with sugar. Combine with vodka. Serve over crushed ice.

Rosella Royale

5ml rosella extract
25ml Davidson plum purée
5ml plum liqueur
sparkling wine

Combine rosella syrup, Davidson plum purée, plum liqueur. Top with sparkling wine

Native mint

The species most often referred to as native mint or Australian mint is one of the mint bushes indigenous to the area just north of Sydney and through the Central Coast.

It is a woodland species with an incredibly aromatic oil even though the plant itself is sparsely leaved - a little like chervil. The leaves are so fine and low in moisture that they dry rapidly and so Australian mint is generally supplied as a dry herb.

Its flavour profile is a cross between a menthol eucalyptus with a suggestion of tom cat when the fresh leaves are crushed through to a delicious beefy note when in very low concentration in food.

In fact, it is extremely appealing in marinades for fetta cheese, in sausages and in pasta.

Braised veal shank

with native mint drizzled pink eye potatoes

The slow wet cooking really does the trick in tenderizing the veal and it's great with the Alpine Pepper and subtle flavour from the paperbark. ***MM***

serves 6

6 boneless veal shanks
12 pink eye potatoes
2 turnips
120g smoked speck or ham
1 roll paper bark
Alpine pepper
2 litres beef or veal stock

1. Pre heat the oven to 150°C
2. heat the stock in a deep roasting tray
3. lay out 6 sheets of paperbark on the bench fibrous side down
5. lay the shank in the center and season with Alpine Pepper
6. cut the turnips into fingers and speck into strips and lay in the center of the shank
7. roll up like a Swiss roll, and tie the ends of the bark and along its length so that it retains its shape
8. place the shanks in the liquid and place in the oven for about 2 hours
9. the best way to test if the shanks are cooked is to pinch them if they feel a little soft they are cooked
10. steam the potatoes
11. infuse some olive oil with native mint the correct ratio is 1 tsp. to 250ml of light olive oil
12. smash the potatoes and drizzle with the mint oil salt and alpine pepper
13. when the shanks have been in the oven for 1½ hours, place the potatoes in too
14. when the shanks are cooked remove them and the potatoes from the tray and rest the meat
15. reduce the stock by half and adjust the seasoning; never add seasoning before you reduce as will concentrate the flavour as it reduces and will get too strong
16. remove the shanks from the paper bark and slice in half

Arrange the potatoes on the plate with the veal shank nearby and finish with the reduced stock.

Kangaroo striploin tartlet
with sweet potato and bush tomato jus

Kangaroo

Kangaroo is a healthy, versatile, lean red meat that is now commonly available throughout the world from animals which are harvested as part of a management plan for the millions of wild animals in Australia.

Kangaroo meat is very low in fat with most of what is present as unsaturated. It could be considered the olive oil equivalent of meat and is also high in protein and iron.

Kangaroo meat is often marinated, cooked rare as with most game meats and rested for as long as it cooks. There's a saying in the industry; "There's no such thing as tough meat, only tough chefs" and this reflects the need for a little care when cooking lean meats.

This is no doubt the easiest recipe in the book and canapés are a great way to introduce new flavours at a cocktail or dinner party. Instead of serving the same old finger foods or boring cheeses, try experimenting with the vast array of native fruits and spices.

Other ideas include asparagus wrapped in emu prosciutto with Wildfire Spice mayonnaise, steamed scallops and desert limes with Alpine Pepper hollandaise or salt and Alpine Pepper squid. ***VC***

serves 8

Makes 20 tartlets

1 kangaroo fillet
200g sweet potato
20g akudjura
80ml game jus
20g Wildfire Spice
20 pastry cases
2g Outback Salt
2g pepper
20g butter
50ml cream

1. Peel and roughly chop the kumara, then place into a small pot together with cold water and a little salt; bring to the boil, then simmer for 35 minutes
2. season the kangaroo fillet with salt and pepper, then sear on a hot grill or BBQ and cook on the hot plate or in an oven until medium rare; season with Wildfire Spice while it rests for as long as it took to cook
3. in a sauce pan combine the ground akudjura with game jus; bring to the boil and simmer, allowing the bush tomato flavour to infuse
4. strain the kumara, then mash and combine with butter and cream

To serve, place a little sweet potato mash in the base of the tart shell, then place a slice of kangaroo on top and finish with a drizzle of bush tomato jus.

Baked Illawarra plum cheesecake

Illawarra plum

The Illawarra plum is an east-coast rainforest tree. The fruit has an external seed and the edible portion is the swollen stem. It has a plum character with a hint of pine and a sticky texture.

The Illawarra plum is a difficult fruit to use due to its tendency to go bitter. To minimise the risk of bitterness avoid using under-ripe fruit or over-cooking. When taste testing sauces or jams do not try them hot. The bitterness often disappears on cooling and absolutely avoid aluminium cookware.

Once mastered, the use of Illawarra plums in sauces and fruit blends produces incomparable results. Classic products are Illawarra plum and chilli sauce, fresh fruit compote, glacé plums and Illawarra plum jam

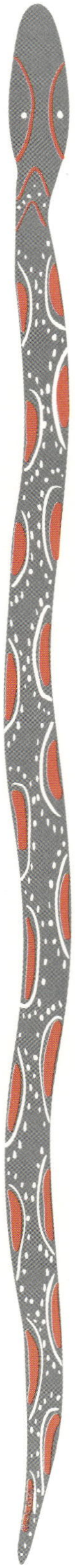

This American dessert favorite is really turned upside down here with the unique flavour of Illawarra plums. The recipe can be varied if you substitute the plums with lemon aspen, riberries, rosella flowers, limes or even Oz Lemon or Fruit Spice. ***BC***

serves 6

185g sweet biscuits
100g butter
100g Illawarra plums
1 tablespoon lemon juice
500g cream cheese
125g castor sugar
3 eggs
100g flour
125ml low fat cream

1. In a food processor pulse the sweet biscuits to crumbs; add melted butter to form the crumb crust
2. in individual ceramic dishes, form the base and edges and set in the fridge for an hour our so
3. wipe out the food processor and blend the Illawarra plums and lemon juice; remove and set aside
4. once again wipe out the blender and combine the cream cheese and sugar together until light and fluffy
5. add the eggs to the mixture, one at a time then add in the flour and cream
6. spoon in the blended Illawarra plum mixture and transfer to the prepared crumb cases
7. bake in at 160°C for 60-70 minutes
8. remove and allow to cool; refrigerate when cool

Serve with rich double cream and fresh fruit garnish (for visuals more than taste).

COOK'S CONVERSION TABLE FOR U.S. AND METRIC

US		Metric
1 teaspoon		5 ml.
1 tablespoon	3 teaspoons	15 ml.
2 tablespoons	1 fluid ounce	30 ml.
4 tablespoons	1/4 cup	60 ml.
5 1/3 tablespoons	1/3 cup	80 ml.
6 tablespoons	3/8 cup	90 ml.
8 tablespoons	1/2 cup	120 ml.
10 2/3 tablespoons	2/3 cup	160 ml.
12 tablespoons	3/4 cup	180 ml.
16 tablespoons	1 cup or 8 ounces	240 ml.
1 cup	1/2 pint or 8 fluid ounces	240 ml. or .236 litre (1/4 litre)
2 cups	1 pint	480 ml.
1 pint	16 ounces	480 ml. or .473 litre
4 1/3 cups	1 quart 2 ounces	1 litre (1,000 millilitres)
1 quart	2 pints	960 ml. or .946 litre
2.1 pints	1.05 quarts or .26 gallons	1 litre
4 quarts	1 gallon	3.785 litres
.035 ounces		1 gram
2.205 pounds		1 kilogram
1 ounce	16 drams	28 grams
1 pound (16 ounces)		453.6 grams
2.20 pounds		1 kilo

Degrees Fahrenheit	Degrees Celsius	Gas Mark	Description
225	110	1/4	Very slow
250	120 / 130	1/2	Very slow
275	140	1	Slow
300	150	2	Slow
325	160 / 170	3	Moderate
350	180	4	Moderate
375	190	5	Moderately hot
400	200	6	Moderately hot
425	220	7	Hot
450	230	8	Hot
475	240	9	Very hot

Master Recipes

Lemon aspen syrup and sauce

Makes 60ml

100ml water
100g sugar
20ml lemon aspen juice
white wine vinegar
your choice of flavours: soy sauce, chilli, ginger, basil, Oz Lemon etc

To make the syrup
1. Begin by heating the water in a saucepan adding the sugar and stirring to dissolve it
2. once the sugar is fully dissolved, add the lemon aspen juice
3. heat to 75°C for 20 minutes, pour into bottles and cap to sterilize the syrup for storage

To make the sauce
1. Pour 50ml of the lemon aspen syrup into a bowl and add vinegar by the teaspoonful, tasting with each addition
2. the flavour will start sweet and then the vinegar will lessen the sweetness with each addition; as a guide, the 50ml will probably take 2 teaspoonfuls to reach an appropriate sweet and sour level for a sauce
3. once this stage has been reached, add the flavour you wish:

   * soy is added dropwise
   * chilli is a simple addition for heat
   * ginger is best by the drop of juice from grated root and
   * 6 leaves of basil would be adequate but they need to be bruised to release the aromatics

Basic mayonnaise

Makes 300ml

200ml vegetable oil
3 egg yolks
1 teaspoon Dijon mustard
juice of 1 lemon
¼ teaspoon Outback salt

1. Whisk the egg yolks in a large bowl; when combined add the mustard; continue to whisk briskly
2. take a tea towel and roll it up, then shape it into a circle on the bench to fit the base of the bowl to make whisking easier
3. gradually pour the oil into the egg mix, whisking continuously; this can also be conveniently done in a food processor
4. as the mixture thickens, add a little lemon juice to thin it out, then add more oil
5. when the mixture has taken all the oil, add the salt

Index

Acknowledgements

This book could not have been compiled without the efforts of three groups of Australians:

Firstly, the people of the 600 Aboriginal Nations who belonged to this land and whose culture and lifestyles so suited this country that we still have access to so many indigenous species of edible plants even after 230 years of land abuse through inappropriate agriculture.

Secondly, we acknowledge the input of the team of chefs and cooks who contributed recipes to this book. They are central to the core story of this book (and the television show) in that they embody our contemporary Australian cuisine and simultaneously, are representatives of the various venues in which we filmed for our television show, Dining Downunder™. They are each mentioned in their respective chapters and we urge you to eat at their restaurants or seek them out wherever they may have moved.

And third, are our sponsors and to be cliché; we couldn't have done this without them. In order to add value to what we bring to the table (no pun intended) we would like to direct you to our sponsor's pages which are a lift out at the back of every copy of this book and also on-line at our informative website at **www.dining-downunder.com.** We refer you to these companies, not simply because of our relationship but they are an elite group of companies with a chauvinistic bent. They are either fully Australian owned and operated or have significant productions here in Australia and necessarily, leave all or a significant proportion of their profits here to foster their continued growth and benefit our local economy. Please support them and when preparing the dishes in this book and shopping for ingredients, please remember their brands and buy their superior products.

As you would imagine, both, the production of a cookbook and a television series are challenging in terms of time, effort and money and we would like to acknowledge the contributions of some special people:

Geordie McRae continually went above and beyond the call of duty and his digital photography and book design are evident throughout this work. His abilities are clearly, only surpassed by his propensity for wattleseed pavlova.

It is unusual for authors to acknowledge co-authors as there is little value in a discourse of mutual admiration. However, in regards to Benjamin Christie, one can only be impressed by his productivity, motivation and drive and his inherent computing and organizational abilities. Benjamin led the assault on the development of the show's website, food service promotions and the book preparation and planning, all as secondary activities to an already more than full-time commitment with his consultancy to Best Restaurants of Australia. Thanks heaps, Mate.

Craig Dangar is another lynch pin in the overall Dining Downunder project and we thank him for his contribution in arranging much needed finance at some very trying times.

And lastly, on a personal note, I would like to acknowledge the patience and guidance of my wife, Clare. She shares the consequences of the financial risk and yet her support, wisdom and understanding is encapsulated in her urgings through somewhat stressful periods; "You do know that you could be having fun with all of this?" "It's just as well that it's your favourite subject." Thanks, Sweetie.

Vic Cherikoff